The
Bodhisattva
Vow

Also by Geshe Kelsang Gyatso

Meaningful to Behold
Clear Light of Bliss
Buddhism in the Tibetan Tradition
Heart of Wisdom
Universal Compassion
The Meditation Handbook
Joyful Path of Good Fortune
Guide to Dakini Land
Heart Jewel
Great Treasury of Merit
Introduction to Buddhism
Understanding the Mind
Tantric Grounds and Paths
Ocean of Nectar
Essence of Vajrayana
Living Meaningfully, Dying Joyfully
Eight Steps to Happiness
Transform Your Life

Profits received from the sale of
this book will be donated to the
NKT-International Temples Project
A Buddhist Charity Building for World Peace
UK email: kadampa@dircon.co.uk
US email: info@kadampacenter.org

GESHE KELSANG GYATSO

The
Bodhisattva Vow

THE ESSENTIAL PRACTICES OF
MAHAYANA BUDDHISM

THARPA PUBLICATIONS
Ulverston, England
Glen Spey, NY, USA

First published in 1991
Second edition reset and revised 1995
Reprinted 1998, 2003

The right of Geshe Kelsang Gyatso
to be identified as author of this work
has been asserted by him in accordance with
the Copyright, Designs, and Patents Act 1988.

Tharpa Publications
Conishead Priory
Ulverston
Cumbria LA12 9QQ, England

Tharpa Publications
47 Sweeney Road
P.O. Box 430
Glen Spey, NY 12737, USA

Cover painting of Buddha Shakyamuni
by Gen Kelsang Wangchen.
Frontispiece painting of the Thirty-five Confession Buddhas
by Gen Kelsang Wangchen.
Cover design by Tharpa Publications.
Cover photo of Geshe Kelsang Gyatso by Kathia Rabelo.
Line illustrations by Sarah Young.

Library of Congress Control Number: 2003100129

British Library Cataloguing in Publication Data
A catalogue record for this book is available
from the British Library.

ISBN 0 948006 49 8 – papercase
ISBN 0 948006 50 1 – paperback

Set in Palatino by Tharpa Publications.
Printed on acid-free 250-year longlife paper and bound
by Cromwell Press, Trowbridge, Wiltshire, England.

Contents

Illustrations

Acknowledgements

Our profound thanks go once again to Venerable Geshe Kelsang Gyatso, the author of *The Bodhisattva Vow*, for his inexhaustible great kindness to Dharma students around the world in writing this book. Long may we continue to merit the author's realized and expert guidance along the spiritual path.

We also thank all the dedicated, senior Dharma students who assisted the author with the rendering of the English and who prepared the final manuscript for publication.

Through the merits created in producing this work, may all living beings find the happiness they seek.

Roy Tyson,
Administrative Director,
Manjushri Mahayana
Buddhist Centre,
July 1995.

Introduction

The subject of this book is the Bodhisattva's moral discipline. The Sanskrit term *Bodhisattva* is the name given to anyone who, motivated by great compassion, has generated bodhichitta, which is a spontaneous wish to attain Buddhahood for the benefit of all living beings. Since everyone has within their mental continuum the seeds of great compassion and bodhichitta, and since everyone can at some time meet a Mahayana Dharma Teacher, it is possible for everyone to become a Bodhisattva by training in the Mahayana teachings.

The Bodhisattva's moral discipline is a higher moral discipline, and it is the main path that leads to the ultimate happiness of great enlightenment. In general, moral discipline is a virtuous determination to abandon any non-virtuous action. For example, if by seeing the disadvantages of killing, stealing, or sexual misconduct we make a firm decision to refrain from such actions, this is moral discipline. Similarly, the determination to refrain from lying, divisive speech, hurtful speech, idle gossip, covetousness, malice, and holding wrong views is also moral discipline.

In *Pratimoksha Sutra*, Buddha says that it would be better for us to die than to break our moral discipline, because death destroys only this one life, whereas breaking our moral discipline destroys our opportunity to experience happiness in many future lives and condemns us to experience the sufferings of lower rebirths over and over again.

In Buddhist countries, moral discipline is regarded as very important, and it is for this reason that monks and nuns are

1

Buddha Shakyamuni

held in such high esteem. However, it is not only monks and nuns who need to practise moral discipline; everyone needs to practise moral discipline because it is the root of all future happiness. Even if we are a very learned scholar, if we ignore the practice of moral discipline our activities will be unsuccessful and we shall experience many problems in the future. On the other hand, if we conscientiously observe moral discipline, we can solve all our human problems and complete our spiritual practices.

The practice of moral discipline is the main cause of rebirth as a human. If we practise generosity without moral discipline, we shall experience some good results in the future, but not in a human body. For example, we may be reborn as a pet cat or dog that is well cared for. The reason why some animals receive great care from humans is that they practised generosity in previous lives, but the reason why they have taken a lower rebirth is that they broke their moral discipline in previous lives.

If we practise moral discipline by abandoning negative actions, such as killing, with the motivation to obtain human happiness, this moral discipline will protect us from lower rebirth and cause us to be reborn as a human being in the future. If we practise moral discipline with a sincere wish to attain liberation for ourself, or full enlightenment for the sake of all living beings, this is higher moral discipline. There are three types of higher moral discipline: Pratimoksha moral discipline, Bodhisattva moral discipline, and Tantric moral discipline. These types of moral discipline are distinguished by the motivation with which they are practised and the particular downfalls that they abandon. Pratimoksha moral discipline is motivated mainly by the aspiration to attain personal liberation, Bodhisattva moral discipline mainly by bodhichitta, and Tantric moral discipline mainly by special Tantric bodhichitta.

Not every practice of moral discipline entails taking vows. For example, if we realize the many faults of killing and, as a result, make a strong decision to abstain from killing, we are practising moral discipline even though we have not taken a vow. A vow is a virtuous determination to abandon particular faults that is generated in conjunction with a traditional ritual. Just as there are three types of moral discipline, so there are three types of vow: Pratimoksha vows, Bodhisattva vows, and Tantric vows.

'Pratimoksha' means 'personal liberation', and so a Pratimoksha vow is a vow that is motivated mainly by the wish to attain personal liberation. There are eight types of Pratimoksha vow:

(1) Nyennä vows – one-day ordination vows
(2) Genyenma vows – vows of a laywoman
(3) Genyenpa vows – vows of a layman
(4) Getsulma vows – vows of a novice nun
(5) Getsulpa vows – vows of a novice monk
(6) Gelobma vows – preliminary vows taken before becoming a fully ordained nun
(7) Gelongma vows – vows of a fully ordained nun
(8) Gelongpa vows – vows of a fully ordained monk

The first three are lay vows and the remaining five are ordination vows. Buddha gives extensive instructions on the Pratimoksha moral discipline and the Pratimoksha vows in the *Vinaya Sutras*.

This book is concerned principally with the Bodhisattva vows. In *Guide to the Bodhisattva's Way of Life*, Shantideva advises those who want to know about the Bodhisattva vows first to study *Akashagarbha Sutra*, and then, for a more detailed explanation of the daily practices of a Bodhisattva, to read *Compendium of Trainings*. Shantideva explains that those who have taken the Bodhisattva vows should know what the root and secondary downfalls are, how to prevent the vows from degenerating, how to purify downfalls, and how to complete the practice of the Bodhisattva vows. All these are explained in this book.

Once we have taken the Bodhisattva vows, we should strive to prevent them from degenerating by retaking our vows several times each day, and then avoid incurring root or secondary downfalls by relying upon mindfulness, alertness, and conscientiousness.

There are four main causes of the degeneration of the Pratimoksha, Bodhisattva, or Tantric vows, which are known as the 'four doors of receiving downfalls'. These are: not knowing what the downfalls are, lack of respect for Buddha's instructions, strong delusions, and non-conscientiousness.

To close the first door, we should learn what the downfalls are and how they are incurred. This can be done by listening to teachings on the subject or by reading authentic commentaries, such as the instructions given below.

To close the second door, we should try to overcome disrespect by contemplating the following:

Since Buddha is omniscient, knowing all past, present, and future phenomena simultaneously and directly, and since he has great compassion for all living beings without exception, there is no valid reason for developing disrespect towards his teachings. It is only due to ignorance that I sometimes disbelieve them.

To close the third door, we should try to subdue our strong delusions by practising the meditations described in *The Meditation Handbook*. If, by practising Lamrim, we are able always to maintain good intentions such as love, compassion, and bodhichitta, there will be no basis for incurring Pratimoksha or Bodhisattva downfalls; and if, by practising generation stage and completion stage, we overcome ordinary appearances and ordinary conceptions, there will be no basis for incurring Tantric downfalls.

We can close the fourth door, non-conscientiousness, by repeatedly bringing to mind the disadvantages of incurring downfalls and the advantages of pure moral discipline. In this way, we become more conscientious.

In brief, the method for preventing our vows from degenerating is to train in renunciation, bodhichitta, the correct view of emptiness, generation stage, and completion stage. By sincerely practising these, we overcome our ordinary attitudes and control our mind, thereby removing any basis for downfalls.

Receiving the Bodhisattva Vows

There now follows an explanation of the methods for receiving and maintaining the Bodhisattva vows, and for completing the vows and trainings of a Bodhisattva.

THE METHOD FOR RECEIVING AND MAINTAINING THE BODHISATTVA VOWS

The main purpose of practising the Mahayana is to attain Buddhahood to benefit all living beings. To accomplish this aim, we must first generate bodhichitta, and then adopt the Bodhisattva's way of life by receiving and maintaining the Bodhisattva vows.

The bodhichitta that we generate before taking the Bodhisattva vows is called 'aspiring bodhichitta'. This is a mind that aspires to attain enlightenment for the benefit of others but that does not yet engage in the actual practices of the Bodhisattva's training. It is like someone intending to go somewhere but not yet setting out on the journey. After we have taken the Bodhisattva vows, our bodhichitta transforms into engaging bodhichitta. This is a mind that actually engages in the practices that lead to the final destination of Buddhahood.

We must first receive the Bodhisattva vows from a qualified Spiritual Guide. Once we have received them at such a ceremony, we can take them on our own at any time and as often as we wish. When we do so, we visualize the Field for Accumulating Merit in front of us and repeat three

Complete Subduer with the Essence of Vajra

times the promise to keep the moral discipline of a Bodhisattva and to avoid all downfalls by engaging in the practice of the six perfections. We can renew or strengthen this promise by engaging in the following practice.

TAKING THE REFUGE VOWS

We begin by considering the benefits of going for refuge:

(1) *We become a pure Buddhist*
(2) *We establish the foundation for taking all other vows*
(3) *We purify the negative karma that we have accumulated in the past*
(4) *We daily accumulate a vast amount of merit*
(5) *We are held back from falling into the lower realms*
(6) *We are protected from harm inflicted by humans and non-humans*
(7) *We fulfil all our temporary and ultimate wishes*
(8) *We quickly attain the full enlightenment of Buddhahood*

Through contemplating these benefits, we make a strong determination or promise to go for refuge to the Three Jewels until we attain enlightenment. We then recite the following prayer three times:

I and all sentient beings, until we achieve enlightenment,
Go for refuge to Buddha, Dharma, and Sangha.

This is like a pure container into which we now put the nectar of the Bodhisattva vows.

GENERATING BODHICHITTA

We begin by considering the benefits of bodhichitta:

(1) *We enter the gateway to the Mahayana*
(2) *We become a Son or Daughter of the Buddhas*
(3) *We surpass Hearers and Solitary Realizers*
(4) *We become worthy to receive offerings and prostrations from humans and gods*

(5) *We easily accumulate a vast amount of merit*
(6) *We quickly destroy powerful negativities*
(7) *We fulfil all our wishes*
(8) *We are free from harm by spirits and so forth*
(9) *We accomplish all the spiritual grounds and paths*
(10) *We have a state of mind that is the source of peace and happiness for all beings*

Through contemplating these benefits, we make a strong determination or promise to attain Buddhahood for the benefit of all living beings. While concentrating on this determination, we recite the following prayer three times:

Through the virtues I collect by giving and other perfections,
May I become a Buddha for the benefit of all.

MAINTAINING ASPIRING BODHICHITTA
BY MEANS OF RITUAL

To prevent our bodhichitta from degenerating, we make the following promise three times:

From this time forth until I become a Buddha,
I shall keep even at the cost of my life
A mind wishing to attain complete enlightenment
To free all living beings from the fears of samsara and solitary peace.

In this way, we undertake to observe the eight precepts of aspiring bodhichitta. These can be found in Appendix II.

RECEIVING THE BODHISATTVA VOWS

Only by engaging in the Bodhisattva's trainings – the practice of the six perfections – and by avoiding the root and secondary downfalls of the Bodhisattva vows can we fulfil the two aims of our bodhichitta – to attain Buddhahood ourself, and to lead all other beings to that state of ultimate happiness. Realizing this, we make a strong determination or promise to engage in the practice of the six perfections and to avoid the root and secondary downfalls. While concentrating on this determination, we recite the following ritual prayer three times:

O Gurus, Buddhas, and Bodhisattvas
Please listen to what I now say.
Just as all the previous Sugatas
Generated the mind of enlightenment
And accomplished all the stages
Of the Bodhisattva training,
So will I too, for the sake of all beings,
Generate the mind of enlightenment
And accomplish all the stages
Of the Bodhisattva training.

MAINTAINING JOY AND CONSCIENTIOUSNESS

So that we may complete our practice of the Bodhisattva vows, we generate and maintain a feeling of joy and conscientiousness while reciting the following two verses:

Now my life has borne great fruit,
My human life has attained great meaning;
Today I am born into the lineage of Buddha
And have become a Bodhisattva.

All my actions from now on
Shall accord with this noble lineage;
And upon this lineage, pure and faultless,
I shall never bring disgrace.

Going for refuge to the Three Jewels and keeping the commitments of refuge are the foundation of the Bodhisattva vows, and refraining from the root and secondary downfalls is the actual practice of the Bodhisattva vows.

Jewel of Radiant Light

The Downfalls of the Bodhisattva Vows

THE METHOD FOR COMPLETING THE VOWS AND TRAININGS OF A BODHISATTVA

By receiving the Bodhisattva vows, we promise to engage in the trainings of a Bodhisattva, all of which are included in the six perfections. The six perfections are the highway to enlightenment and the downfalls of the Bodhisattva vows are the principal obstacles on the way. Therefore, now that we have taken the vows, we need to emphasize two main practices: to avoid the downfalls of the Bodhisattva vows and to practise the six perfections. These practices will now be explained under the following headings:

1 An explanation of the downfalls of the Bodhisattva vows
2 A method for purifying downfalls
3 The actual trainings of a Bodhisattva

AN EXPLANATION OF THE DOWNFALLS OF THE BODHISATTVA VOWS

The instructions on the downfalls of the Bodhisattva vows include extensive advice on how we should conduct our daily lives by transforming all our actions into the Bodhisattva's way of life. These instructions are extremely important for those who have taken the Bodhisattva vows. By putting them into practice, we shall gradually complete the Bodhisattva's training, and eventually attain the supreme bliss of Buddhahood.

There are forty-six secondary downfalls and eighteen root downfalls. These will now be explained in detail.

The forty-six secondary downfalls

If we incur any of the following secondary downfalls, we damage our Bodhisattva vows but we do not actually break them; just as a small knock may crack, but not break, a cup.

1 Not making offerings to the Three Jewels every day By taking the Bodhisattva vows, we commit ourself to making offerings to the Three Jewels every day. These can be physical offerings, such as material gifts or gestures of respect; verbal offerings, such as praises; or mental offerings of faith. If a day passes without our making any of these three types of offering, we incur a secondary downfall. This commitment advises us that we need to accumulate merit every day by making physical, verbal, or mental offerings to the Three Jewels.

2 Indulging in worldly pleasures out of attachment Whenever we enjoy pleasures such as food, drink, clothing, or music, we should try to do so while maintaining bodhichitta motivation. If we fail to do this, and indulge in such pleasures simply out of attachment or discontent, we incur a secondary downfall. This commitment advises us that we should transform our daily activities into the Bodhisattva's way of life by continuously maintaining bodhichitta motivation.

3 Being disrespectful to those who received the Bodhisattva vows before us By showing disrespect to a practitioner who received the Bodhisattva vows before us, we incur a secondary downfall. This commitment advises us that we need to respect senior Bodhisattva Sangha in order to increase our merit.

4 Not replying to others If someone greets us in a friendly and courteous manner, and without a good reason we give no reply, we incur a secondary downfall. This commitment advises us that we should try to make others' minds happy by giving suitable answers and advice.

5 Not accepting invitations If someone with a good motivation invites us to dinner, to a party, or for an outing, and without a good reason we decline merely out of pride, laziness, or anger, we incur a secondary downfall. Valid reasons for declining invitations include: we are ill, we do not have the free time, it would make others unhappy, there would be a danger or obstacle to our Dharma practice, and so on. This commitment advises us that, in accepting invitations, we should make a dedication prayer that the host's generosity becomes a cause for all living beings to experience the enjoyments of a Buddha.

6 Not accepting gifts If we are given gold, money, or other gifts, and without a good reason we refuse them merely out of pride, anger, or laziness, we incur a secondary downfall. This commitment advises us that, in accepting offerings from others, we should use them in the most meaningful way.

7 Not giving Dharma to those who desire it If someone with a sincere desire to practise Dharma requests us to teach them, and without a good reason we refuse merely out of laziness, we incur a secondary downfall. Valid reasons for not teaching include: we do not know the subject well enough, it is not suitable to teach them, it would make others unhappy, we are ill, we do not have the free time, and so on. This commitment advises us that, whenever we have the chance, we should try to eliminate the darkness of ignorance from the minds of others by giving Dharma teachings.

Powerful King of the Nagas

8 Forsaking those who have broken their moral discipline
We incur a secondary downfall if we ignore, with a judgemental or self-righteous attitude, those who have broken their moral discipline. This commitment advises us that we should keep the intention to help all living beings, including those who have broken their moral discipline.

9 Not acting in ways that cause others to generate faith To help others effectively, it is necessary to conduct ourself in a way that causes them to develop confidence in us. If we fail to do this, but instead retain bad habits that are likely to attract criticism, such as drinking or smoking, we incur a secondary downfall. This commitment advises us that we should keep pure discipline sincerely, and show a good example so as to increase others' faith in us. In this way, they will derive great results from our teachings.

10 Doing little to benefit others An austere, solitary lifestyle is appropriate for Hinayanists because their principal objective is to renounce attachment and thereby attain their own liberation. However, a Mahayanist should not needlessly diminish his or her capacity to help others by shunning wealth, reputation, or involvement with other people. If we do this without a special, altruistic motivation, we incur a secondary downfall. This commitment advises us that, if we have bodhichitta motivation, we can increase our wealth and reputation, providing we use it solely to bring increased benefit to living beings.

11 Not believing that Bodhisattvas' compassion ensures that all their actions are pure Buddha taught that since higher Bodhisattvas have abandoned self-cherishing and are motivated only by compassion, all their actions, even killing, stealing, and so forth, are free from negativity. If we refuse to believe this, we incur a secondary downfall. This commitment advises us that we should rejoice in all Bodhisattvas' actions, and that we too should be motivated solely by compassion and bodhichitta.

As with the preceding eleven secondary downfalls, each of the remaining thirty-five carries with it some special advice. Although the advice relating to the remaining downfalls is not explicitly indicated below, we should try to understand what it is as we contemplate each downfall.

12 Acquiring wealth or fame through wrong livelihood Some people, desirous of wealth, praise, respect, and so forth, resort to dishonest means to acquire it. They pretend to be special, holy people, outwardly showing good behaviour, talking smoothly, flattering others, praising the possessions of others while subtly hinting that they need such things themselves, or giving small presents in the hope of receiving larger presents in return. If, with selfish motives, we behave in such a way, we incur a secondary downfall.

13 Indulging in frivolity If, without a good reason but motivated only by excitement, attachment, or non-conscientiousness, we indulge in frivolous activities such as singing, dancing, playing, or meaningless conversation, we incur a secondary downfall.

14 Claiming that Bodhisattvas need not abandon samsara Some people, misunderstanding what samsara is, assert that Bodhisattvas need not abandon samsara or delusions, but can attain enlightenment in the midst of samsara while working for the welfare of sentient beings. If we hold this view and encourage others to think the same, we incur a secondary downfall because such views interfere with our spiritual progress.

15 Not avoiding a bad reputation If we unnecessarily engage in actions that cause us to receive criticism or a bad reputation, we incur a secondary downfall. However, if our actions benefit many beings, cause the pure Buddhadharma to flourish, or are necessary to preserve the integrity of our moral discipline, it does not matter if a few people criticize us.

16 Not helping others to avoid negativity If we have the ability and the opportunity to help someone avoid committing negative actions, but without a good reason fail to do so, we incur a secondary downfall.

17 Retaliating to harm or abuse If, out of anger or impatience, we repay abuse with abuse, beating with beating, criticism with criticism, and so on, we incur a secondary downfall.

18 Not apologizing when we have the opportunity If we have disturbed another person by acting in an unskilful way, and later the opportunity to apologize arises but, out of pride or laziness, we fail to do so, we incur a secondary downfall.

19 Not accepting others' apologies If someone who has previously harmed us later apologizes and, without a good reason but not out of resentment, we refuse to accept his or her apology, we incur a secondary downfall. If we do so out of resentment we incur a root downfall.

20 Making no effort to control our anger Sometimes, because of strong habits of anger or because of difficult circumstances, we find ourself getting angry. If at such times we do not make a special effort to practise patience, we incur a secondary downfall.

21 Gathering a circle of followers out of desire for profit or respect If, for selfish reasons, we try to gather students, disciples, or followers, we incur a secondary downfall.

22 Not trying to overcome laziness We have promised to attain Buddhahood for the sake of all living beings, but to accomplish this requires great effort. If we do not try to eliminate our laziness, or our attachment to sleep and other worldly pleasures, we incur a secondary downfall.

23 Indulging in senseless conversation out of attachment If we spend much of our time doing this, we incur a secondary downfall.

Leader of the Heroes

24 Neglecting to train in mental stabilization The attainment of tranquil abiding is essential if we wish to attain profound realizations. If we fail to make an effort to listen to and think about the instructions on tranquil abiding, or to improve our concentration by training in tranquil abiding, we incur a secondary downfall.

25 Not overcoming obstacles to mental stabilization In this context, there are five obstacles to mental stabilization, or concentration:

(1) Needless self-reproach and excitement
(2) Malicious thoughts
(3) Sleep and dullness
(4) Distracting desires
(5) Frequent and disturbing doubts

If we make no effort to abandon these, we incur a secondary downfall.

26 Being preoccupied with the taste of mental stabilization Here, the 'taste' of mental stabilization is the experience of bliss, peace, and suppleness induced by concentration. If we become attached to this, and regard it as the ultimate result of concentration, we incur a downfall because this attachment diminishes our wish to help others and hinders our Mahayana practice. The real value of concentration is not the temporary bliss that it induces, but its being the means by which higher realizations can be attained.

27 Abandoning the Hinayana The teachings and practices of the Hinayana are methods to release beings from the sufferings of samsara; therefore, they are holy Dharma and objects to be respected. If we regard them as contradictory to the Mahayana and believe that they must be abandoned, we incur a secondary downfall.

28 Studying the Hinayana to the detriment of our Mahayana practice To attain bodhichitta and other Mahayana

realizations, and finally to accomplish the state of Buddhahood, we need to study and practise the Mahayana teachings. If, instead of doing this, we put great effort into
studying the Hinayana, with the result that our Mahayana
practice is weakened, we incur a secondary downfall.

29 Studying non-Dharma subjects without a good reason
If we study non-Dharma subjects so as to increase our capacity to help other beings, this will not interfere with our
Mahayana practice; but, if we study non-Dharma subjects
without a good reason, we incur a secondary downfall.

**30 Becoming engrossed in non-Dharma subjects for their
own sake** Sometimes we may begin to study non-Dharma
subjects for good reasons, but gradually become so engrossed
in them that we lose sight of our original intentions and
end up studying them simply for pleasure. The result of
this is likely to be that we shall lose the energy we have
for Dharma study and practice. If we allow this to happen,
we incur a secondary downfall. This downfall applies as
much to the study of academic non-Dharma subjects as it
does to more practical subjects.

31 Criticizing other Mahayana traditions Within the Mahayana, there is a great variety of different traditions, and
each tradition has its own texts and practices. If some of these
appear to be contrary to our own tradition, we should not
discriminate against them or criticize them without a good
reason. If we do so with a deluded motivation, we incur a
secondary downfall.

32 Praising ourself and scorning others This is similar to
the first root downfall, except that here we are motivated
by slight pride but have no intention to deceive others.

33 Making no effort to study Dharma Listening to
Dharma teachings and reading Dharma books are the
lamps that dispel the darkness of ignorance. If, without a

good reason, we make no effort to do either, we incur a secondary downfall.

34 Preferring to rely upon books rather than upon our Spiritual Guide The root of Dharma realizations is sincere reliance upon our Spiritual Guide. If we neglect this practice and prefer to acquire our understanding from books, we incur a secondary downfall.

35 Not going to the assistance of those in need If someone asks for our help, or we realize that he hopes for it, and we are in a position to help him, and yet out of laziness or some other delusion we do not go to his assistance, we incur a secondary downfall. For example, if someone asks to be shown the way, or asks for practical or spiritual help, or requests us to mediate in a dispute, we should assist in whatever way we can.

36 Neglecting to take care of the sick If we show no concern for sick people or animals whom we encounter, and do not do our best to help them, we incur a secondary downfall.

37 Not acting to dispel suffering Whenever we see humans who are physically or mentally handicapped, or insane, or whenever we see animals, we should feel compassion and consider how we can help them. If we are unable to be of any practical assistance, we should at least pray for them. If we do nothing, we incur a secondary downfall.

38 Not helping others to overcome their bad habits If we meet people who habitually engage in behaviour that directly or indirectly harms themselves or others, and we have the opportunity skilfully to help them overcome these habits, we should do so. If we cannot help them directly, we should at least pray for them. If we do nothing, we incur a secondary downfall. This downfall differs from the sixteenth secondary downfall in that the former concerns specific, heavy negative actions, whereas this one concerns

Glorious Pleasure

frequently repeated but otherwise relatively minor unskilful actions, such as smoking, drinking, petty theft, or acting in ways that cause disharmony.

39 Not returning help to those who benefit us We should always remember the kindness of those who benefit us, and maintain the intention to repay them. If we completely forget their kindness, we incur a secondary downfall.

40 Not relieving the distress of others If we meet people who are beset with grief, and we have the opportunity to comfort them and yet do nothing, we incur a secondary downfall.

41 Not giving to those who seek charity When beggars or others in need of our charity approach us, we must try to give them something. If we refuse for some invalid reason other than miserliness, we incur a secondary downfall. If we refuse out of miserliness, we incur a root downfall.

42 Not taking special care of disciples If we have disciples, we must help them by guiding them along the spiritual path and, as far as we are able to, provide them with whatever they need for their Dharma practice. If we do not take special care of our faithful disciples, we incur a secondary downfall.

43 Not acting in accordance with the inclinations of others When relating to others, we should try to please them by conforming with their wishes whenever possible, unless of course their wishes are wrong and would lead to great suffering. If we ignore the wishes of others without a good reason, we incur a secondary downfall.

44 Not praising the good qualities of others If we see someone whose conduct is a good example for our Dharma practice, we should rejoice in his good qualities and praise him. If, motivated by envy, pride, jealousy, or some other delusion, we do not praise him, we incur a secondary downfall.

Jewel Fire

45 Not doing wrathful actions when appropriate There are times when it is necessary to resort to wrathful methods, such as speaking in a very forceful manner, to prevent someone committing negative actions or to subdue his or her pride. If we realize clearly that such a time has come, and we know that our wrathful action will greatly benefit him in the future, we incur a secondary downfall if, for some incorrect reason, we do not carry out that action.

46 Not using miracle powers, threatening actions, and so forth When we perform wrathful actions, we should use whatever miracle powers we have, otherwise we shall incur a secondary downfall. However, many realized Teachers such as Je Tsongkhapa have said that the time for displaying miracle powers has now passed because these days people are likely to think that we are engaging in black magic, with the result that Buddhadharma will be brought into disrepute and our own safety may be threatened. Therefore, we should follow the example of the Kadampa Geshes such as Dromtönpa, Geshe Potowa, and Je Tsongkhapa. Though they possessed potent miracle powers, they never displayed them. Outwardly, they always remained like ordinary people, never claiming to be in any way special. They lived among ordinary people and helped them principally by encouraging them to cultivate love, compassion, and bodhichitta, and by teaching them all the stages of the path to enlightenment. Nowadays, this is the most useful way for Bodhisattvas to act.

The eighteen root downfalls

The root downfalls are more serious than the secondary downfalls because, if we incur a root downfall, we actually break our Bodhisattva vows, whereas, if we incur a secondary downfall, we damage our vows but we do not completely break them.

Jewel Moonlight

Altogether there are eighteen root downfalls, which are explained in *The Bodhisattvas' Grounds* by Asanga and *Compendium of Trainings* by Shantideva. Although only eighteen are enumerated, each root downfall has many different aspects.

1 Praising ourself and scorning others We incur a root downfall if we praise ourself with the motivation of deceiving others so that we might receive gifts or enhance our reputation. We also incur a root downfall if we criticize others with the wish to hurt them. In both cases, the downfall is complete only if someone hears and understands our words.

2 Not giving wealth or Dharma If someone asks us to give material help such as financial assistance, or spiritual help such as teachings or Dharma books, and we are in a position to oblige but out of miserliness refuse, we incur a root downfall.

3 Not accepting others' apologies If someone who has physically or verbally harmed us later apologizes and we refuse to accept his or her apology, preferring to harbour a grudge, we incur a root downfall.

4 Abandoning the Mahayana If we reject any Mahayana scripture that teaches either the vast path or the profound path, claiming that it is not Buddha's teaching, we incur a root downfall. It is also a downfall to propagate views that contradict Dharma, and to encourage others to practise such false teachings.

5 Stealing the property of the Three Jewels We incur a root downfall if we steal anything that has been offered to the Three Jewels.

6 Abandoning Dharma We incur this downfall if we criticize any of Buddha's Hinayana or Mahayana teachings, declaring that they are not Buddhadharma and therefore should not be practised.

Meaningful to Behold

7 Taking away saffron robes This downfall can be incurred only by those in positions of power in monastic communities. Should such people, with a bad motivation, expel monks or nuns from the monastery by taking back their robes, they incur a root downfall, even if those whom they expel have previously broken their ordination vows.

8 Committing the five heinous actions These actions are killing one's father, killing one's mother, killing a Foe Destroyer, maliciously wounding a Buddha, and causing a schism within the Sangha.

9 Holding wrong views We incur a root downfall if we hold wrong views denying the law of karma, the existence of past and future lives, or other truths that we need to believe in order to attain liberation.

10 Destroying places such as towns We incur a root downfall if, with a bad motivation, we wilfully destroy a place of habitation or an environment.

11 Explaining emptiness to those who are likely to misunderstand We incur a root downfall if we teach emptiness in an unskilful way and cause those who are listening to develop serious and harmful misunderstandings.

12 Causing others to abandon the Mahayana If we cause Mahayana practitioners to give up their bodhichitta by telling them that they will never become a Buddha because the practice of the six perfections is beyond their capacity, and advise them to enter the less demanding Hinayana path by which liberation is swiftly attained, we incur a root downfall.

13 Causing others to abandon the Pratimoksha We incur a root downfall if we cause an ordained person to give up his or her Vinaya practice by saying that the Vinaya is a Hinayana practice that is not relevant to the Mahayana path.

14 Belittling the Hinayana We incur a root downfall if we have a disrespectful opinion of the Hinayana path, maintaining that it does not lead to actual liberation.

15 Speaking falsely about profound emptiness If we lack a correct understanding of emptiness, and yet teach emptiness to others claiming with a selfish motivation that we have a direct realization of emptiness, we incur a root downfall.

16 Accepting property that has been stolen from the Three Jewels We incur this downfall if we accept goods that we know to have been stolen from the Three Jewels. For example, some money may have been offered to a Dharma community for a puja or for the publication of Dharma books. If someone appropriates this money and then offers a portion of it to us, and we accept with full knowledge that it has been stolen, we incur a root downfall.

17 Making bad rules Those in charge of spiritual communities incur this downfall if they make rules that unnecessarily interfere with pure Dharma practice, for example by organizing the community in such a way that business activities take precedence over the practice of meditation.

18 Giving up bodhichitta If, due to self-cherishing or discouragement, we give up our bodhichitta motivation, we incur a root downfall and destroy the foundation of our Mahayana realizations.

To incur a root downfall, four binding factors must be present:

(1) Not regarding the action as wrong
(2) Not wishing to abstain from the action in the future
(3) Rejoicing in the action
(4) Having no sense of shame or consideration for others

For example, if we praise ourself in the hope of deceiving others into giving us money, we create the action of the first root downfall, but, if we immediately recognize that we have done wrong, we shall not incur the actual root downfall. Likewise, if we immediately regret the action, feel ashamed or embarrassed by it, or develop the intention never to repeat it, we shall not incur the complete downfall. This applies to all the other root downfalls except the ninth and the eighteenth. To incur these downfalls, it is not necessary for the four binding factors to be present; just by adopting wrong views or giving up bodhichitta we incur a root downfall.

To avoid incurring the root and secondary downfalls, it is essential to know what they are; therefore, as soon as we have taken the Bodhisattva vows, we should make a determined effort to learn them and commit them to memory. We should try to understand each downfall, think about how we might come to incur it, and make plans to avoid such situations.

It is important to be skilful in our approach to the vows. We should not have unrealistic expectations or make promises that we cannot keep. Instead, we should adopt the Bodhisattva's way of life gradually. Each of the vows can be kept on many levels. For example, we have a vow to abandon the obstacles to developing concentration, but it is impossible to abandon all these obstacles at once. First we should try to avoid gross distractions, and then gradually strive to abandon the subtle interferences. All the Bodhisattva vows are aspects of the practice of the six perfections. Until we attain enlightenment, we need continually to improve our practice of the six perfections, and in this way gradually deepen the level at which we are able to keep the vows.

When a Teacher gives the Bodhisattva vows, he or she should explain them well. He should not encourage his disciples to promise to keep all the vows perfectly from the start. Moreover, from their side, the disciples should not make over-enthusiastic promises, pledging to keep all the vows faultlessly without even knowing what they are. Such disciples will break their vows the very next day. After taking the Bodhisattva vows, an intelligent disciple will first learn what they involve. Then he will resolve to keep each one to the best of his ability, and gradually improve his practice of the Bodhisattva moral discipline.

The advice to keep the vows gradually does not mean that we can temporarily put to one side the vows that we do not like. We have to work with all the vows, gradually improving the way we observe them. For example, as our miserliness decreases, we shall be able to keep the vows relating to giving more purely, and, as our anger decreases, we shall be able to keep those relating to patience more purely. Thus, we should begin to practise all the vows as soon as we have taken them, practise them to the best of our ability, and never lose the determination to keep them perfectly in the future.

A Method for Purifying Downfalls

In our previous lives, while under the influence of deluded minds, we created a great deal of negative karma, and we also transgressed our commitments and incurred root and secondary downfalls. As a result, we now experience difficulties in developing faith and conviction in Dharma, and in making progress on the stages of the path to enlightenment. Since these transgressions and downfalls seriously obstruct our spiritual development, it is essential that we purify them.

In *Akashagharba Sutra*, Buddha says that those who have incurred root downfalls of the Bodhisattva vows should generate strong regret, and at the dawn of each day face east and sincerely make offerings and prostrations to the Bodhisattva Akashagharba while reciting his name. That Bodhisattva will then appear in various aspects, either directly in front of the practitioner or in his or her dreams. He will then purify their downfalls, and the practitioner will attain powerful concentration and a strong realization of mindfulness.

One of the best methods for purifying downfalls, however, is recommended by Shantideva in *Guide to the Bodhisattva's Way of Life*, where he advises us:

I should practise the *Sutra of the Three Heaps*
Three times each day and three times each night,
And, with reliance on the Three Jewels and
    bodhichitta,
Purify non-virtues and downfalls.

Jewel Moon

Here, the *'Three Heaps'* refers to the *Mahayana Sutra of the Three Superior Heaps*, or *The Bodhisattva's Confession of Moral Downfalls*, the root text of which now follows.

MAHAYANA SUTRA OF THE THREE SUPERIOR HEAPS

Namo: *The Bodhisattva's Confession of Moral Downfalls*

I, whose name is . . . , at all times go for refuge to the Guru, go for refuge to the Buddha, go for refuge to the Dharma, go for refuge to the Sangha.

To the Teacher, Blessed One, Tathagata, Foe Destroyer, Completely Perfect Buddha, Glorious Conqueror Shakyamuni I prostrate.

To the Tathagata Complete Subduer with the Essence of Vajra I prostrate.

To the Tathagata Jewel of Radiant Light I prostrate.

To the Tathagata Powerful King of the Nagas I prostrate.

To the Tathagata Leader of the Heroes I prostrate.

To the Tathagata Glorious Pleasure I prostrate.

To the Tathagata Jewel Fire I prostrate.

To the Tathagata Jewel Moonlight I prostrate.

To the Tathagata Meaningful to Behold I prostrate.

To the Tathagata Jewel Moon I prostrate.

To the Tathagata Stainless One I prostrate.

To the Tathagata Bestower of Glory I prostrate.

To the Tathagata Pure One I prostrate.

To the Tathagata Transforming with Purity I prostrate.

Stainless One

To the Tathagata Water Deity I prostrate.

To the Tathagata God of Water Deities I prostrate.

To the Tathagata Glorious Excellence I prostrate.

To the Tathagata Glorious Sandalwood I prostrate.

To the Tathagata Endless Splendour I prostrate.

To the Tathagata Glorious Light I prostrate.

To the Tathagata Glorious One without Sorrow
I prostrate.

To the Tathagata Son without Craving I prostrate.

To the Tathagata Glorious Flower I prostrate.

To the Tathagata Clearly Knowing through Enjoying
Pure Radiance I prostrate.

To the Tathagata Clearly Knowing through Enjoying
Lotus Radiance I prostrate.

To the Tathagata Glorious Wealth I prostrate.

To the Tathagata Glorious Mindfulness I prostrate.

To the Tathagata Glorious Name of Great Renown
I prostrate.

To the Tathagata King of the Victory Banner, Head of
the Powerful Ones I prostrate.

To the Tathagata Glorious One Complete Subduer
I prostrate.

To the Tathagata Great Victor in Battle I prostrate.

To the Tathagata Glorious One Complete Subduer
Passed Beyond I prostrate.

To the Tathagata Glorious Array Illuminating All
I prostrate.

Bestower of Glory

To the Tathagata Jewel Lotus Great Subduer I prostrate.

To the Tathagata, Foe Destroyer, Completely Perfect
Buddha, King of Mount Meru Seated Firmly on
a Jewel and a Lotus I prostrate.

O All you [Tathagatas] and all the others, however many
Tathagatas, the Foe Destroyers, the Completely Perfect
Buddhas, the Blessed Ones there are dwelling and abiding
in all the worldly realms of the ten directions, all you
Buddhas, the Blessed Ones, please listen to me.

In this life and in all my lives since beginningless time,
in all my places of rebirth whilst wandering in samsara, I
have done negative actions, have ordered them to be done,
and have rejoiced in their being done. I have stolen the property of the bases of offering, the property of the Sangha,
and the property of the Sanghas of the ten directions, have
ordered it to be stolen, and have rejoiced in it being stolen.
I have committed the five unbounded heinous actions,
have ordered them to be committed, and have rejoiced in
their being committed. I have completely engaged in the
paths of the ten non-virtuous actions, have ordered others
to engage in them, and have rejoiced in their engaging in
them.

Being obstructed by such karmic obstructions, I shall
become a hell being, or I shall be born as an animal, or I
shall go to the land of the hungry ghosts, or I shall be born
as a barbarian in an irreligious country, or I shall be born
as a long-life god, or I shall come to have incomplete senses, or I shall come to hold wrong views, or I shall have no
opportunity to please a Buddha.

All such karmic obstructions I declare in the presence of
the Buddhas, the Blessed Ones, who have become exalted
wisdom, who have become 'eyes', who have become witnesses, who have become valid, who see with their wisdom. I confess without concealing or hiding anything, and
from now on I shall avoid and refrain from such actions.

Pure One

All you Buddhas, the Blessed Ones, please listen to me. In this life and in all my previous lives since beginningless time, in all my places of rebirth whilst wandering in samsara, whatever root of virtue there is in my giving to others, even in my giving a morsel of food to one born as an animal; whatever root of virtue there is in my maintaining moral discipline; whatever root of virtue there is in my actions conducive to great liberation; whatever root of virtue there is in my acting to fully ripen sentient beings; whatever root of virtue there is in my generating a supreme mind of enlightenment; and whatever root of virtue there is in my unsurpassed exalted wisdom; all of these assembled, gathered, and collected together, by fully dedicating them to the unsurpassed, to that of which there is no higher, to that which is even higher than the high, and to that which surpasses the unsurpassed, I fully dedicate to the unsurpassed, perfect, complete enlightenment.

Just as the Buddhas, the Blessed Ones of the past, have dedicated fully, just as the Buddhas, the Blessed Ones who are yet to come, will dedicate fully, and just as the Buddhas, the Blessed Ones who are living now, dedicate fully, so too do I dedicate fully.

I confess individually all negative actions. I rejoice in all merit. I beseech and request all the Buddhas. May I attain the holy, supreme, unsurpassed, exalted wisdom.

Whoever are the Conquerors, the supreme beings living now, those of the past, and likewise those who are yet to come, with a boundless ocean of praise for all your good qualities, and with my palms pressed together I go close to you for refuge.

This concludes the Mahayana Sutra entitled *Sutra of the Three Superior Heaps.*

Transforming with Purity

AN EXPLANATION OF THE PRACTICE

This has three parts:

1 An introduction to the practice
2 The visualization
3 The actual practice

AN INTRODUCTION TO THE PRACTICE

This Sutra is included within the *Collection of Precious Jewels Sutra* (Tib. *könchog tsegpa*). It is called *Sutra of the Three Superior Heaps* because it contains three 'heaps' or collections of virtue: prostration, purification, and dedication.

In this practice, we visualize the Thirty-five Confession Buddhas and practise purification in their presence. In general, all Buddhas have the power to protect living beings from suffering and negative karma, but, because of the prayers and dedications they made while they were Bodhisattvas, these Thirty-five Buddhas have a special karmic link with the humans of this world. Through the power of their blessings and prayers, we can swiftly purify even the heaviest negative actions simply by faithfully reciting their names.

Any living being, even a worm or an insect, can commit negative actions, but only humans have the fortune to be able to purify them. We have been accumulating non-virtuous actions and experiencing their suffering results since beginningless time, but we now have the opportunity to purify them completely. We should make use of this precious opportunity to purify our negative karma, not to create more! Since purification is the root of future happiness and spiritual realizations, we should strive to cleanse our mind of delusions and negative karma by engaging in the practice of the *Sutra of the Three Superior Heaps*.

Merely beholding Buddha's body or representations of his body, speech, or mind is immensely beneficial. There

Water Deity

are many true stories that illustrate this. Once at Nalanda Monastery, Chandrakirti developed a strong wish to meet Buddha Avalokiteshvara and so he made fervent requests day and night. Eventually, much to Chandrakirti's delight, Avalokiteshvara appeared directly before him. Wishing to give the local people a chance to see Avalokiteshvara, Chandrakirti requested him to sit on his shoulders while he walked around the town. Knowing that ordinary people did not have sufficiently pure minds to see a Buddha, Avalokiteshvara initially refused, but when Chandrakirti persisted in his requests Avalokiteshvara eventually agreed. Chandrakirti set off through the streets exhorting the people to make prostrations to the Buddha on his shoulders. Most people saw nothing and assumed that Chandrakirti had gone mad, while one person, with particularly heavy karmic obscurations, saw the corpse of a dog on his shoulders! Only one person, an old woman wineseller, saw the actual form of Avalokiteshvara, and she saw only his right foot. Even so, this experience was so powerful that as a result she later attained many profound realizations.

In a previous age, a messenger once took shelter in a temple in which there was a wall-painting of Buddha Kashyapa. Seeing the form of this Buddha, he developed great faith and yearned to see an actual Buddha. As a result, he later took a human rebirth as Shariputra, one of Buddha Shakyamuni's foremost disciples, and attained liberation in that life.

A wild boar was once being chased through a forest by a hunter. Just as it was at the point of collapse, the terrified animal reached a clearing in which stood a stupa, a symbolic representation of Buddha's mind. Overcome by exhaustion, the boar collapsed and died. As a result of seeing the stupa, the boar's mind received Buddha's blessings, and through the power of these blessings it was able to die peacefully and take rebirth in the god realm.

God of Water Deities

Hearing Buddha's speech, or a representation of his speech, or listening to or recalling the name of a Buddha, is just as beneficial. For example, there was once a pigeon that used to listen to Vasubandhu while he recited the Sutras. As a result of the blessings the pigeon received from hearing the sound of the Sutras, it subsequently took rebirth in the human realm as one of Vasubandhu's disciples and became a very famous scholar called Stirmati.

Through reciting the names of the Thirty-five Buddhas, many of Je Tsongkhapa's disciples received visions of them. The reason we do not see pure beings such as Buddhas and Bodhisattvas is that our minds are obstructed by negative karma and delusions, not because they are not there before us. For example, on an overcast day we cannot see the sun, but this does not mean that the sun does not exist. When we succeed in purifying the cloud-like delusions and negative karma that obscure our mind, we shall be able to see Buddhas directly, and then we shall find it easy to accomplish all the Mahayana realizations.

So as to increase our enthusiasm for purification practices, and our faith and respect for the Buddhas, we should contemplate as follows:

All the problems I have experienced since beginningless time, and all the problems I shall experience in the future, result from my negative karma. Therefore, nothing can be more beneficial than to practise purification sincerely.

Buddhas are perfect witnesses to confession. Through the power of their blessings, it is possible to purify all the negative karma I have accumulated since beginningless time. This opportunity to engage in purification is solely due to the kindness of the Buddhas.

THE VISUALIZATION

In the space in front of us we visualize Buddha Shakyamuni seated on a jewelled throne supported by eight white

Glorious Excellence

elephants, which symbolize the power of purification. He sits in the vajra posture on cushions of a lotus, a moon, and a sun. The lotus symbolizes renunciation, the moon symbolizes bodhichitta, and the sun symbolizes wisdom directly realizing emptiness.

Buddha wears the saffron robes of a fully ordained monk. Serene and majestic, his bearing is that of one who has passed beyond all worldly concerns. Gracing his crown is an ushnisha, demonstrating that he has always regarded his Spiritual Guide as supreme. His left hand rests in his lap in the gesture of meditative equipoise and holds a begging bowl filled with nectar, which reveals his transcendence of death, delusions, and the torment of an impure body and mind. The middle finger of his right hand touches the ground, calling the earth to witness his victory over the Devaputra demons. He smiles gently, his clear eyes gazing at us with the love of a father for his dearest child. He is fearless like the king of the lions, and his radiance dispels the fears of all who behold him.

His golden body is made of light and is resplendent with the thirty-two signs and eighty indications of a fully enlightened being. Like a universal sun, his brilliance pierces the clouds of ignorance obscuring the minds of living beings. His deep and melodious voice reverberates throughout infinite worlds, ripening seeds of virtue and revealing liberating paths. His purified mind abides eternally in the tranquil ocean of reality, seeing all phenomena as clearly as a jewel held in the hand, and suffused with an all-embracing compassion. He is the ultimate refuge of all living beings.

In front of Buddha Shakyamuni are the remaining thirty-four Buddhas, seated in five rows. In the first row, closest to Buddha Shakyamuni, are the first six Buddhas: Complete Subduer with the Essence of Vajra, Jewel of Radiant Light, Powerful King of the Nagas, Leader of the Heroes, Glorious Pleasure, and Jewel Fire, arranged from left to right as we look at them. In front of these, and lower still,

Glorious Sandalwood

are the next seven Buddhas: Jewel Moonlight, Meaningful to Behold, Jewel Moon, Stainless One, Bestower of Glory, Pure One, and Transforming with Purity. In front of these, and slightly lower, are the seven Buddhas: Water Deity, God of Water Deities, Glorious Excellence, Glorious Sandalwood, Endless Splendour, Glorious Light, and Glorious One without Sorrow. In front of these are the seven Buddhas: Son without Craving, Glorious Flower, Clearly Knowing through Enjoying Pure Radiance, Clearly Knowing through Enjoying Lotus Radiance, Glorious Wealth, Glorious Mindfulness, and Glorious Name of Great Renown. Finally, in the row nearest to us are the remaining seven Buddhas: King of the Victory Banner Head of the Powerful Ones, Glorious One Complete Subduer, Great Victor in Battle, Glorious One Complete Subduer Passed Beyond, Glorious Array Illuminating All, Jewel Lotus Great Subduer, and King of Mount Meru. All these Buddhas sit on jewelled thrones on cushions of a lotus, a moon, and a sun. This assembly of Thirty-five Confession Buddhas is surrounded by all the Buddhas and Bodhisattvas of the ten directions.

We should regard each Buddha's body as the synthesis of all Sangha Jewels, each Buddha's speech as the synthesis of all Dharma Jewels, and each Buddha's mind as the synthesis of all Buddha Jewels. It does not matter if we cannot perceive the visualization clearly; the important thing is to generate deep faith and to have no doubt that we are actually in the presence of real, living Buddhas.

We should know the name of each Buddha, the world over which he presides, his colour, his hand gestures, the objects that he holds, and the particular negative karma that is purified by reciting his name. The hand gestures and the objects held by each Buddha can be learned by studying the drawings in this book. The remaining features are listed in the chart on pages 76-8.

Endless Splendour

THE ACTUAL PRACTICE

The actual practice of the *Sutra of the Three Superior Heaps* is explained in three parts:

1 Purifying non-virtuous actions
2 Dedicating virtue
3 Conclusion

Purifying non-virtuous actions

Most of the non-virtuous actions that we have committed since beginningless time are included within the ten non-virtuous actions: killing, stealing, sexual misconduct, lying, divisive speech, hurtful speech, idle gossip, covetousness, malice, and holding wrong views. These are explained in detail in *Joyful Path of Good Fortune*. We have to purify all these non-virtues, together with all our downfalls of the Pratimoksha, Bodhisattva, and Tantric vows.

It is impossible to alter the fact that a negative action has been committed, but it is possible to eradicate the potential of a negative action to produce suffering. Every non-virtuous action has four potentials, each of which has its own effect: the ripened effect, the environmental effect, the effect that is an experience similar to the cause, and the effect that is a tendency similar to the cause. A detailed explanation of these four effects can be found in *Joyful Path of Good Fortune*. To purify these four potentials, Buddha taught the four opponent powers, which are all contained within this Sutra.

The first opponent power, the power of reliance, purifies the potential for the environmental effect, and also functions to subdue negative karma in general. The second opponent power, the power of the opponent force, purifies the potential for the ripened effect, and also functions as the direct opponent to negative karma in general. The third opponent power, the power of regret, purifies the potential

Glorious Light

for the effect that is an experience similar to the cause, and also functions to prevent the power of negative karma from increasing. The fourth opponent power, the power of promise, purifies the potential for the effect that is a tendency similar to the cause, and also prevents us from repeating the action. The degree to which we succeed in purifying negative karma depends upon our skill in applying these four opponent powers.

From this we can understand that sincerely going for refuge to the Three Jewels, even without an intention to purify, functions to subdue our negative karma, and to weaken the potential to experience an unpleasant environmental effect. For example, we may be born in hell as a consequence of not having purified the ripened effect of a severely negative action, but the duration of our stay there will be shortened if we have previously gone for refuge. Similarly, if we commit a negative action and then immediately generate regret, although regret by itself does not have the power to purify the action completely, it will prevent the power of the action increasing, and also weaken its potential to produce an experience similar to the cause.

The way to apply the four opponent powers within the practice of the *Sutra of the Three Superior Heaps* will now be explained under the following four headings:

1 The power of reliance
2 The power of the opponent force
3 The power of regret
4 The power of promise

The power of reliance

Focusing our mind on the visualized assembly of Thirty-five Buddhas, and recognizing them as the essence of all Buddha Jewels, Dharma Jewels, and Sangha Jewels, we generate deep faith and go for refuge while reciting the following lines from the Sutra:

Glorious One without Sorrow

I, whose name is . . . , at all times go for refuge to the Guru, go for refuge to the Buddha, go for refuge to the Dharma, go for refuge to the Sangha.

While we are reciting this, we should also mentally generate bodhichitta, thinking: 'I must attain Buddhahood for the sake of all mother sentient beings.'

The power of the opponent force

With the strong faith and conviction we developed by going for refuge, we now make physical prostrations while reciting the name of each Buddha as a request for them to purify our negative karma. There are three ways to make physical prostrations: making full-length prostrations by prostrating our whole body on the ground, making half-length prostrations by kneeling respectfully and touching our palms and our forehead to the ground, or making a gesture of respect such as pressing our palms together at our heart.

Prostrations are a powerful method for purifying negative karma, disease, and obstacles, and for increasing our merit, our happiness, and our Dharma realizations. Temporarily, prostrations improve our physical health, and ultimately they cause us to attain a Buddha's Form Body. A more extensive explanation of the benefits of prostrations can be found in *Joyful Path of Good Fortune*.

When we make prostrations to the Thirty-five Confession Buddhas, we can either make one prostration to each Buddha as we recite his name, and then repeat the cycle as many times as we wish, or we can make a number of prostrations, say seven, twenty-one, fifty, or a hundred, to the first Buddha while reciting his name, and then go on to make the same number of prostrations to the second Buddha, and so on. If we do this we shall probably not be able to complete the prostrations to all the Thirty-five Buddhas in one session, in which case we simply begin the next session where we left off.

Son without Craving

Each Buddha's name has great meaning. There is not the space here to explain the meaning of all the names, but it may be helpful to understand the meaning of Buddha Shakyamuni's name. The Tibetan for 'Tathagata' is *deshin shegpa*, in which *deshin* means 'ultimate truth', or emptiness, and *shegpa* means 'gone'. Thus, *deshin shegpa* is a mind that has gone into, or completely mixed with emptiness; in other words it is the Wisdom Truth Body. Therefore, 'Tathagata' means that Buddha has attained the Wisdom Truth Body and the Nature Body. 'Foe Destroyer' indicates that Buddha has completely destroyed the obstructions to liberation. 'Completely Perfect Buddha' affirms that he has attained great enlightenment, and also indicates that he has attained the clear light of bliss and the illusory body. He is called 'Glorious' because he is the Protector of living beings, and 'Conqueror' because he is victorious over the four maras. 'Muni' means 'Able One', and indicates that Buddha has the ability to free all living beings from the ocean of samsara. Since Buddha was born to the Shakya clan, he is called 'Shakyamuni'. All these titles, except 'Shakya', apply equally to all Buddhas. By contemplating these names, we come to understand the good qualities of the Buddhas, and thereby strengthen our faith.

The power of regret

After reciting the names of the Buddhas together with making prostrations, we can either continue to prostrate, or sit down while we recite the rest of the Sutra. We recall that the Thirty-five Buddhas are in the space in front of us surrounded by all the Buddhas and Bodhisattvas of the ten directions. By reciting the following words from the Sutra, we ask them to give us their attention and witness our confession:

Glorious Flower

O All you [Tathagatas] and all the others, however many Tathagatas, the Foe Destroyers, the Completely Perfect Buddhas, the Blessed Ones there are dwelling and abiding in all the worldly realms of the ten directions, all you Buddhas, the Blessed Ones, please listen to me.

We now acknowledge that in the past we have committed many heavy negative actions, and with great remorse confess them as follows:

In this life and in all my lives since beginningless time, in all my places of rebirth whilst wandering in samsara, I have done negative actions, have ordered them to be done, and have rejoiced in their being done. I have stolen the property of the bases of offering, the property of the Sangha, and the property of the Sanghas of the ten directions, have ordered it to be stolen, and have rejoiced in it being stolen. I have committed the five unbounded heinous actions, have ordered them to be committed, and have rejoiced in their being committed. I have completely engaged in the paths of the ten non-virtuous actions, have ordered others to engage in them, and have rejoiced in their engaging in them.

Here, the 'property of the bases of offering' is anything that has been offered to the Three Jewels. It includes offerings and donations for pujas; for the construction of temples or other buildings used by Dharma communities; for statues, paintings, or stupas; or for the publication of Dharma books – in short, anything that has been offered to or that belongs to a Dharma community. Stealing from a Dharma Centre is extremely heavy negative karma that causes rebirth in hell or one of the other unfree states. The 'property of the Sangha' is the belongings of individual Dharma practitioners, and the 'property of the Sanghas of the ten directions' is anything that belongs to the ordained

Clearly Knowing through Enjoying Pure Radiance

Sangha community. The 'five unbounded heinous actions', otherwise known as the 'five actions of immediate retribution' or the 'five heinous actions', are killing one's father, killing one's mother, killing a Foe Destroyer, maliciously wounding a Buddha, and causing a schism within the Sangha. Harming our Spiritual Guide is equivalent to the fourth, and deliberately causing a division within a Dharma community is equivalent to the fifth. We have committed actions such as these many times in previous lives, and may even have done them in this life. Acknowledging this, we should try to generate strong regret by contemplating the fate that awaits us if we fail to purify these actions. We recite the following lines from the Sutra:

Being obstructed by such karmic obstructions, I shall become a hell being, or I shall be born as an animal, or I shall go to the land of the hungry ghosts, or I shall be born as a barbarian in an irreligious country, or I shall be born as a long-life god, or I shall come to have incomplete senses, or I shall come to hold wrong views, or I shall have no opportunity to please a Buddha.

These lines remind us that an effect of negative karma is rebirth in one of the eight unfree states. The meaning of the last line is that we shall have no opportunity to meet, or to please, a Spiritual Guide.

Having acknowledged the extent of our negative karma, we now practise a special method for purifying it. At our heart, we visualize all the potentials of our negative actions in the form of a black letter PAM (depicted on page 118). We then imagine that the negative karma of all other living beings gathers in the aspect of smoke and dissolves into the PAM, and we think that the PAM has become the essence of all our own and others' negativity. We pray:

65

Clearly Knowing through Enjoying Lotus Radiance

**All such karmic obstructions I declare in the presence
of the Buddhas, the Blessed Ones, who have become
exalted wisdom, who have become 'eyes', who have
become witnesses, who have become valid, who see
with their wisdom. I confess without concealing or
hiding anything, . . .**

Then we imagine that white wisdom lights and nectars
descend from the hearts of all the Thirty-five Buddhas and
enter our body through our crown. When they reach the PAM,
they completely destroy it, just as a light destroys darkness
as soon as it is switched on. We firmly believe that all our
negative karma created since beginningless time has been
purified. The wisdom lights pervade our body and mind,
increasing our life span, our good fortune, our physical
and mental power, and our Dharma realizations.

Buddhas 'have become exalted wisdom' because they
know the entire past, present, and future directly; and they
'have become 'eyes'' because they watch all living beings
with eyes of great compassion. Since Buddhas know everything, and in particular because they are aware of the good
and bad actions we have done in this and previous lives,
they 'have become witnesses'. They 'have become valid'
because they are non-deceptive objects of refuge; and they
'see with their wisdom' all the negative karma that we
have committed in the past, as well as the suffering that
will result from it.

The power of promise

Unless we refrain from negative actions in the future, it
will be impossible to purify fully those we have already
committed. If we think that it does not matter if we continue to commit negative actions because we have a method
for purifying them, this shows that we do not understand
purification. In *Lion's Roar Sutra* Buddha says that he has
taught the Dharma of the *Three Superior Heaps* to enable us

Glorious Wealth

to purify negative karma, but those who continue to perform negative actions thinking that they can purify them later are foolish. Therefore, we must refrain from nonvirtuous actions by making the following promise to the Buddhas:

. . . and from now on I shall avoid and refrain from such actions.

Some practitioners can promise to refrain from every downfall and negative action for the rest of their lives, and by relying upon mindfulness, conscientiousness, and alertness never break this promise. If we are not yet able to make such a promise, we should first promise to refrain from all negative actions for one week, for example, and then gradually extend the duration of our restraint to a month, a year, and so on, until we can promise to refrain for the rest of our life. It is important to keep whatever promises we have made to the Buddhas and to our Spiritual Guide because broken promises are serious obstacles to our spiritual progress.

Dedicating virtue

Generally, dedication ensures that virtuous actions produce great results. Here, we dedicate so that our practice will definitely produce great and powerful results in the future. We begin by requesting the Buddhas to witness our dedication:

All you Buddhas, the Blessed Ones, please listen to me.

Then we review the virtuous actions to be dedicated:

In this life and in all my previous lives since beginningless time, in all my places of rebirth whilst wandering in samsara, whatever root of virtue there is in my giving to others, even in my giving a morsel of

Glorious Mindfulness

food to one born as an animal; whatever root of virtue there is in my maintaining moral discipline; whatever root of virtue there is in my actions conducive to great liberation; whatever root of virtue there is in my acting to fully ripen sentient beings; whatever root of virtue there is in my generating a supreme mind of enlightenment; and whatever root of virtue there is in my unsurpassed exalted wisdom; all of these assembled, gathered, and collected together, . . .

The first two types of virtue mentioned here, giving and moral discipline, are self-explanatory. The third, 'actions conducive to great liberation', refers to the remaining four perfections – patience, effort, mental stabilization, and wisdom – which are the means to attain the great liberation of Buddhahood. 'Acting to fully ripen sentient beings' refers to the four ways of gathering disciples. Whereas the virtues just listed principally function to ripen our own mental continuum, the four ways of gathering disciples principally function to ripen others' mental continuums. 'Generating a supreme mind of enlightenment' refers to the generation of bodhichitta, and 'unsurpassed exalted wisdom' refers to any spiritual realization of a person on an actual Hinayana or Mahayana path. If we have not yet developed spontaneous renunciation or bodhichitta, we do not possess such exalted wisdom, but we can appreciate the exalted wisdom of others and dedicate their virtues. 'All of these assembled' means the collection of all our own virtues produced by these actions, 'gathered' refers to the collection of all other beings' virtues, and 'collected together' refers to our own and others' virtues united together. All of this is what is to be dedicated. As for the purpose for which it is dedicated, the Sutra continues:

. . . by fully dedicating them to the unsurpassed, to that of which there is no higher, to that which is even higher than the high, and to that which surpasses

Glorious Name of Great Renown

the unsurpassed, I fully dedicate to the unsurpassed, perfect, complete enlightenment.

Just as the Buddhas, the Blessed Ones of the past, have dedicated fully, just as the Buddhas, the Blessed Ones who are yet to come, will dedicate fully, and just as the Buddhas, the Blessed Ones who are living now, dedicate fully, so too do I dedicate fully.

The 'unsurpassed' refers to a Buddha's Form Body, which arises from unsurpassed merit; 'that of which there is no higher' refers to a Buddha's Truth Body, which arises from the highest wisdom; 'even higher than the high' refers to a Buddha's Emanation Bodies, which are even higher than Hinayana Foe Destroyers to whom they give teachings; and 'that which surpasses the unsurpassed' refers to a Buddha's Enjoyment Body, which surpasses Superior Bodhisattvas, who themselves are unsurpassed by any other sentient being. In short, by reciting this dedication prayer we dedicate all the virtues of ourself and others to the attainment of a Buddha's Form Body and a Buddha's Truth Body so that we shall be able to benefit all living beings.

The benefits of this dedication can be understood by considering the effects of a simple action such as giving. If we do not make any dedication at all, it is probable that the potential to produce happiness created by our virtuous action of giving will soon be destroyed by anger or wrong views. This danger can be avoided by dedicating the virtue for some mundane purpose. If we do this, we shall experience a beneficial effect such as wealth in the future, but, as soon as this is used up, the positive potential of our original action will also have been exhausted. However, if we make the supreme dedication as mentioned in this Sutra, the potential power of that simple act of giving will never be exhausted, no matter how much we enjoy its temporary fruits. For example, if a drop of water is taken from a spring and put into an ocean it will not evaporate until the ocean itself dries up. In a similar fashion, if we dedicate our virtue of giving to full enlightenment, it will not be exhausted until enlightenment is attained. Therefore, its results are infinite. The same applies to all other virtues. All the Buddhas of the past dedicated in this way while they were Bodhisattvas, and now they are experiencing the beneficial results of their dedication. We should follow their example and dedicate in the same way.

Conclusion

We continue the recitation of the Sutra with a brief prayer:

I confess individually all negative actions. I rejoice in all merit. I beseech and request all the Buddhas. May I attain the holy, supreme, unsurpassed, exalted wisdom.

Confession purifies negative karma in general, rejoicing purifies negativities caused by jealousy, beseeching Buddhas not to pass away purifies actions that disturb our Spiritual Guide, and requesting them to turn the Wheel of Dharma purifies the negative action of abandoning Dharma. The virtues of this short prayer are dedicated to the attainment of the holy, supreme, unsurpassed, exalted wisdom, in other words Buddha's omniscient wisdom.

The last lines of the Sutra explicitly teach refuge in the Buddhas of the three times, and implicitly reveal refuge in Dharma and Sangha:

Whoever are the Conquerors, the supreme beings living now, those of the past, and likewise those who are yet to come, with a boundless ocean of praise for all your good qualities, and with my palms pressed together I go close to you for refuge.

The essential meaning of these lines is that the practice of the three superior heaps – prostration, purification, and dedication – should be combined with refuge in the Three Jewels.

The best way to avoid committing negative actions or incurring downfalls is always to maintain a good heart through the practice of the twenty-one meditations explained in *The Meditation Handbook*; and the best method for purifying negative actions and downfalls already accumulated is to practise, the *Sutra of the Three Superior Heaps*. With these two practices, we shall be able to safeguard the whole of our Bodhisattva's way of life.

NAME	WORLD	COLOUR	PURIFIES
Buddha Shakyamuni	Unforgetting World (this world)	Golden	All the negative actions accumulated over 10,000 aeons
Complete Subduer with the Essence of Vajra	Essence of Space (above this world)	Blue	All the negative actions accumulated over 10,000 aeons
Jewel of Radiant Light	Adorned with Jewels (east)	White	All the negative actions accumulated over 25,000 aeons
Powerful King of the Nagas	Pervaded by Nagas (south-east)	Blue	All the negative actions accumulated over eight aeons
Leader of the Heroes	Pervaded by Heroes (south)	Yellow	Negative karma of speech
Glorious Pleasure	Joyful (south-west)	Orange	Negative karma of mind
Jewel Fire	Pervaded by Light (west)	Red	Causing a schism within the Sangha
Jewel Moonlight	Excellent Light (north-west)	White	All the negative actions accumulated over one aeon
Meaningful to Behold	Sound of the Drum (north)	Green	Criticizing Superior beings
Jewel Moon	Adorned with Light Rays (north-east)	White	Killing one's mother
Stainless One	Pervaded by Dust (below this world)	Smoke-coloured	Killing one's father
Bestower of Glory	The Glorious (above this world)	White	Killing a Foe Destroyer

NAME	WORLD	COLOUR	PURIFIES
Pure One	Unobstructed (east)	Orange	Maliciously wounding a Buddha
Transforming with Purity	Sorrowless (south-east)	Yellow	All the negative actions accumulated over 10,000 aeons
Water Deity	Stainless (south)	Blue	Raping nuns or Foe Destroyers
God of Water Deities	Perfectly Clear (south-west)	White	Killing Bodhisattvas
Glorious Excellence	Blissful (west)	Red	Killing Learner Superiors
Glorious Sandalwood	Pervaded by Fragrance (north-west)	Orange	Stealing from the Sangha
Endless Splendour	Possessing Vitality (north)	Red	Destroying stupas
Glorious Light	Meaningful (north-east)	White	Negative actions committed out of hatred
Glorious One without Sorrow	Unobstructed (below this world)	Pale blue	Negative actions committed out of attachment
Son without Craving	Free from Attachment (above this world)	Blue	All the negative actions accumulated over 10,000 aeons
Glorious Flower	Increasing Flowers (east)	Yellow	All the negative actions accumulated over 100,000 aeons
Clearly Knowing through Enjoying Pure Radiance	Pervaded by Brahmas (south-east)	White	All the negative actions accumulated over 1,000 aeons

NAME	WORLD	COLOUR	PURIFIES
Clearly Knowing through Enjoying Lotus Radiance	Adorned with Lotuses (south)	Red	All the negative actions accumulated over seven aeons
Glorious Wealth	Adorned with Jewels (south-west)	Pink	Negativity arising from bad habits
Glorious Mindfulness	Perfectly Clear (west)	Yellow	Negative karma of body
Glorious Name of Great Renown	Signless (north-west)	Green	Displeasing Buddhas
King of the Victory Banner	Clear Sense Power (north)	Yellow	Negative actions committed out of jealousy
Glorious One Complete Subduer	Enjoyment (north-east)	White	Commanding others to commit negative actions
Great Victor in Battle	Without Delusion (below this world)	Black	Negative actions committed out of pride
Glorious One Complete Subduer Passed Beyond	The Glorious (east)	White	Slander
Glorious Array Illuminating All	Adorned with Light (south)	Yellow	Rejoicing in evil
Jewel Lotus Great Subduer	The Glorious (west)	Red	Abandoning Dharma
King of Mount Meru	Jewel (north)	Clear blue	Breaking commitments

Training in the Six Perfections

THE ACTUAL TRAININGS OF A BODHISATTVA

Maintaining the Bodhisattva vows is the basis for the actual trainings of the Bodhisattva. These are all included within the practice of the six perfections: the perfections of giving, moral discipline, patience, effort, mental stabilization, and wisdom. If we wish to become enlightened, but do not practise the six perfections, we are like someone who wants to go somewhere but does not actually set out on the journey.

THE PERFECTION OF GIVING

Giving is a virtuous mental intention to give, or a bodily or verbal action of giving that is motivated by a virtuous state of mind. Giving practised with bodhichitta motivation is a perfection of giving. There are three types of giving:

1 Giving material things
2 Giving Dharma
3 Giving fearlessness

Giving material things

To practise giving material things, we first contemplate the disadvantages of miserliness and the benefits of giving, and then we engage in the actual practice of giving to others. In the *Condensed Perfection of Wisdom Sutra*, Buddha teaches that miserliness leads to poverty and rebirth as a

King of the Victory Banner

hungry ghost. Even in this life, miserliness causes us suffering. It is a tight, uncomfortable mind that leads to isolation and unpopularity. Giving, on the other hand, is a joyful mind that leads us to experience wealth and abundant resources in the future.

There is no point in clinging to our possessions, for wealth acquires meaning only when it is given away or used to benefit others. Since without any choice we shall have to part with all our possessions when we die, it is better to part with them now and thereby derive some benefit from having owned them. Moreover, if at the time of our death we have strong attachment to our possessions, this will prevent us from having a peaceful death, and may even prevent us from taking a fortunate rebirth.

When we go on holiday, we take care to carry enough money to see us through the whole holiday, but how much more important it is to ensure that we travel to future lives with enough virtue, or merit, to provide us with all the resources we shall need. Our practice of giving is the best insurance against future poverty.

We should give away our possessions only when the time is right; that is, when it would not cause any hindrances to our spiritual practice or endanger our life, and when the person to whom we are giving will derive some significant benefit. Otherwise, we should not give away our possessions even if someone asks for them. For example, if we can see that a gift will cause harm to others, we should not offer it. We need to consider all the implications of our action, including how it will affect others besides the person who is to receive the gift. We also need to keep those things that are necessary for our Dharma practice. If we were to give these away, we would be indirectly harming others because we would be creating obstacles to our progress towards enlightenment for their sake.

We should mentally dedicate all our possessions to others, but we should physically give them away only when it is most suitable to do so. This skilful way of thinking is, in itself, a form of giving. For example, charitable organisations do not immediately give away everything that is donated to them, but keep a certain amount in reserve for when it is most needed. Even so, while they are holding on to the money, they do not consider it to be their own; they simply think that they are looking after it for others until a need arises. If we view all our possessions in a similar way, we shall be practising giving all the time.

The amount of merit we accumulate through the practice of giving depends upon several factors besides the actual value of the gift. One factor is the nature of the recipient. There are three classes of being to whom it is especially meritorious to give: holy beings, such as our Spiritual Guide, Buddhas, and Bodhisattvas; those who have shown us great kindness, such as our parents; and those who are in great need, such as the poor, the sick, and the handicapped. Another important factor is our motivation. It is more meritorious to put a few crumbs on a bird table with a motivation of pure compassion than it is to give a diamond ring out of attachment. The best motivation, of course, is bodhichitta. The virtue created by giving with this motivation is limitless.

Giving Dharma

There are many ways to give Dharma. If, with a good motivation, we teach even just one word of Dharma to others, we are giving Dharma. This is much more beneficial than any kind of material gift because material things help others only in this life, whereas the gift of Dharma helps them in this and all their future lives. There are many other ways in which we can give Dharma – for example, by dedicating our virtue so that all living beings may enjoy peace and happiness, or by whispering mantras into the ears of animals.

Giving fearlessness

To give fearlessness is to protect other living beings from fear or danger. For example, if we rescue someone from a fire or from some other natural disaster, if we protect others from physical violence, or if we save animals and insects who have fallen into water or who are trapped, we are practising giving fearlessness. If we are not able to rescue those in danger, we can still give fearlessness by making prayers and offerings so that they may be released from danger. We can also practise giving fearlessness by praying for others to become free from their delusions, especially the delusion of self-grasping, which is the ultimate source of all fear.

THE PERFECTION OF MORAL DISCIPLINE

Moral discipline is a virtuous mental determination to abandon any fault, or it is a bodily or verbal action motivated by such a determination. Moral discipline practised with bodhichitta motivation is a perfection of moral discipline. There are three types of moral discipline:

1 The moral discipline of restraint
2 The moral discipline of gathering virtuous Dharmas
3 The moral discipline of benefiting living beings

The moral discipline of restraint

This is the moral discipline of abstaining from non-virtue. To practise this moral discipline, we need to understand the dangers of committing negative actions, make a promise or vow to abandon them, and then keep that promise or vow. Simply failing to commit negative actions unintentionally is not a practice of moral discipline because it is not motivated by a determination to abstain.

Any spiritual discipline that avoids or overcomes either mental faults or negative actions of body or speech is

Glorious One Complete Subduer

included within the moral discipline of restraint. For example, if we understand the dangers of the ten non-virtuous actions, promise to refrain from them, and keep that promise, we are practising the moral discipline of restraint.

Sometimes we can take vows by ourself by recognizing the faults of the actions we want to abandon and promising to refrain from them for whatever length of time we can. Even if we promise to refrain from just one negative action for only a short time – for example, if we promise only to abandon killing for just one week – and we keep that promise, we are practising the moral discipline of restraint. However, as our capacity increases we should gradually extend the duration of our restraint, and also promise to abandon other non-virtuous actions.

To practise moral discipline, we need to rely upon mindfulness, alertness, and conscientiousness. Mindfulness prevents us from forgetting our vows, alertness keeps a check on our mind and warns us if delusions are about to arise, and conscientiousness protects our mind from non-virtue. For example, we may be in a situation, such as a lively party, in which it would be easy to incur the Bodhisattva downfall of praising ourself and scorning others. However, if we practise mindfulness, we shall constantly remember that we have promised not to do such things, and there will be no danger of our incurring this downfall out of forgetfulness. Similarly, if we maintain alertness, we shall be able to detect delusions such as pride or envy as soon as they begin to arise, and then use conscientiousness to check their development.

When we take the Bodhisattva vows, we must have the intention to keep them continuously until we are enlightened. If we are to fulfil our wish to attain enlightenment quickly for the sake of others, we need to overcome our faults as soon as we can. For a Bodhisattva, the main object to be abandoned is the intention to work solely for one's own sake. Bodhisattvas see clearly the dangers of self-cherishing – thinking oneself to be supremely important – and they realize that it is the principal obstacle to developing bodhichitta and to attaining enlightenment. In the *Condensed Perfection of Wisdom Sutra*, Buddha says that the moral discipline of a Bodhisattva does not degenerate if he or she enjoys beautiful forms, sounds, tastes, or other objects of the senses, but if a Bodhisattva develops concern for his own welfare, both his moral discipline and his bodhichitta degenerate. If we generate bodhichitta and later think that it would be better to seek only our own liberation, we incur a root Bodhisattva downfall and break our moral discipline of restraint.

With the motivation of bodhichitta, no action can be non-virtuous because bodhichitta eliminates self-cherishing, which is the root of all non-virtuous actions. Even if a Bodhisattva has to kill, this action is not non-virtuous because it is performed solely for the benefit of all living beings. Although others may condemn them, Bodhisattvas incur no negative karma when they perform such actions because their bodhichitta ensures that all their actions are pure. This is illustrated by an episode from a previous life of Buddha Shakyamuni, while he was still a Bodhisattva. At that time, he was the captain of a ship that was ferrying five hundred merchants on a special voyage. With his clairvoyance, he saw that one of the merchants was planning to kill all the others. Seeing that as a result of this the merchant would be reborn in hell, he generated great compassion for him and for his intended victims. He decided to take upon himself the karma of killing rather than allow all five hundred merchants to suffer and so, with pure bodhichitta motivation, he killed the wicked merchant. In this way, he protected that merchant from a hellish rebirth and saved the lives of all the others. As a result of this action of killing, that Bodhisattva made great spiritual progress.

The moral discipline of gathering virtuous Dharmas

We practise this moral discipline when we sincerely practise any virtuous action, such as keeping the Bodhisattva vows purely, practising the six perfections, making offerings to the Three Jewels, or putting energy into studying, meditating on, or propagating holy Dharma.

The moral discipline of benefiting living beings

This is the moral discipline of helping others in whatever way we can. If we cannot offer practical help to someone, we can at least make prayers for him or her and maintain a continuous intention to give assistance when an opportunity arises. We can understand how to practise this moral discipline by studying the instructions on the last twelve secondary downfalls of the Bodhisattva vows.

When we help others, we should be tactful and sensitive. We should try to understand the other person's experience and point of view, and then offer help that is relevant to him, and in such a way that he can accept it. We cannot help others if we attack their values and beliefs or if we ignore their temperament and their personal circumstances. We have to adapt our own behaviour so that it suits the other person and makes him feel at ease. Instead of imposing our own moral standards on others and passing judgement on them if they do not comply, we should simply act in the way that will have the most positive effect. We need both flexibility of mind and flexibility of behaviour.

Since Bodhisattvas have great compassion, they do whatever is necessary to help others. In effect, Bodhisattvas will do whatever needs to be done to make someone else happy because when others are happy their minds are more open and receptive to advice and example. If we wish to influence others, we can do so only if we do not antagonize them or make them feel uncomfortable or frightened.

Great Victor in Battle

The tact and sensitivity required by a Bodhisattva when helping others is well illustrated by an episode from the life of the great Tibetan Teacher, Geshe Langri Tangpa. A woman who had recently given birth to a baby girl was frightened that she would lose her baby because she had already given birth to one child who had died in infancy. The woman expressed her anxiety to her mother, who told her that children given into the care of Geshe Langri Tangpa would not die. Later, when the little girl fell ill, the woman took her to see Geshe Langri Tangpa, but, when she, arrived she found him sitting on a throne giving a discourse to a thousand disciples. The woman began to worry that her child would die before the end of the discourse. She knew that Geshe Langri Tangpa was a Bodhisattva and would show patience, and so she walked up to the throne and, in a loud, affronted tone of voice declared, 'Here, take your baby. Now you look after her!' She turned to the audience and said, 'This is the father of my child', and then turned back to Geshe Langri Tangpa and pleaded softly, 'Please don't let her die.' Geshe Langri Tangpa just nodded his head in acceptance. As if he really were the father of the child, he wrapped it tenderly in his robes and continued his discourse. His disciples were astonished and asked him, 'Are you really the father of that child?' Knowing that if he were to deny it, the woman would have been thought crazy and the people would have ridiculed her, Geshe Langri Tangpa replied that he was.

Although he was a monk, Geshe Langri Tangpa acted like a real father for the child, delighting in her and caring for her. After some time, the mother returned to see if her daughter was well. When she saw how healthy the child was, she asked Geshe Langri Tangpa if she could have her back again. The Geshe then kindly returned the girl to her mother. When his disciples realized what had happened, they said, 'So you are not really the father after all!' and Geshe Langri Tangpa replied, 'No, I am not.' In this way,

Geshe Langri Tangpa responded to the woman's actions with pure compassion and acted in accordance with the needs of the time.

THE PERFECTION OF PATIENCE

Patience is a virtuous mind that is able to bear harm, suffering, or profound Dharma. Patience practised with bodhichitta motivation is a perfection of patience.

We need to cultivate patience even if we have no interest in spiritual development because, without it, we remain vulnerable to anxiety, frustration, and disquiet. If we lack patience, it is difficult for us to maintain peaceful relationships with others.

Patience is the opponent to anger, the most potent destroyer of virtue. We can see from our own experience how much suffering arises from anger. It prevents us from judging a situation correctly, and it causes us to act in regrettable ways. It destroys our own peace of mind and disturbs everyone else we meet. Even people who are normally attracted to us are repelled when they see us angry. Anger can make us reject or insult our own parents, and, when it is intense, it can even drive us to kill the people we love, or even to take our own life.

Usually anger is triggered off by something quite insignificant, such as a comment that we take personally, a habit that we find irritating, or an expectation that was not fulfilled. Based on such small experiences, anger weaves an elaborate fantasy, exaggerating the unpleasantness of the situation, and providing rationalizations and justifications for the sense of disappointment, outrage, or resentment. It leads us to say and do harmful things, thereby causing offence to others and transforming a small difficulty into a great problem.

If we were asked, 'Who caused all the wars in which so many people have died?', we would have to reply that they were caused by angry minds. If nations were full of calm, peace-loving people, how could wars ever arise? Anger is the greatest enemy of living beings. It harmed us in the past, it harms us now, and, if we do not overcome it through the practice of patience, it will continue to harm us in the future. As Shantideva says:

. . . this enemy of anger has no function
Other than to harm me.

External enemies harm us in slower and less subtle ways. If we practise patience with them, we can even win them over and turn them into our friends; but there can be no reconciliation with anger. If we are lenient with anger, it will take advantage of us and harm us even more. Moreover, whereas external enemies can harm us only in this life, anger harms us for many future lives. Therefore, we need to eliminate anger as soon as it enters our mind because, if we do not, it will quickly become a blazing fire that consumes our merit.

Patience, on the other hand, helps us in this life and in all future lives. As Shantideva says:

There is no evil greater than anger
And no virtue greater than patience.

With patience, we can accept any pain that is inflicted upon us, and we can easily endure our usual troubles and indispositions. With patience, nothing upsets our peace of mind and we do not experience problems. With patience, we maintain an inner peace and tranquillity that allows spiritual realizations to grow. Chandrakirti says that if we practise patience we shall have a beautiful form in the future, and we shall become a holy being with high realizations.

There are three types of patience:

1 The patience of not retaliating
2 The patience of voluntarily enduring suffering
3 The patience of definitely thinking about Dharma

Glorious One Complete Subduer Passed Beyond

The patience of not retaliating

To practise this type of patience, we need to remain continuously mindful of the dangers of anger and the benefits of patient acceptance, and, whenever anger is about to arise in our mind, we need immediately to apply the methods for eliminating it. We begin by learning to forbear small difficulties, such as insignificant insults or minor disruptions to our routine, and then gradually to improve our patience until we are able to forbear even the greatest difficulty without getting angry.

When we are meditating on patience, we can use many different lines of reasoning to help us overcome our tendency to retaliate. For example, we can contemplate that if someone were to hit us with a stick, we would not get angry with the stick, because it was being wielded by the attacker and had no choice. In the same way, if someone insults us or harms us, we should not get angry with him, because he is being manipulated by his deluded minds and also has no choice. Similarly, we can think that just as a doctor does not get angry if a feverish patient lashes out at him, so we should not get angry if confused living beings, suffering from the sickness of the delusions, harm us in any way. There are many special lines of reasoning such as these to be found in *Joyful Path of Good Fortune* and *Meaningful to Behold*.

The fundamental reason why we receive harm is that we have harmed others in the past. Those who attack us are merely the conditions whereby our karma ripens; the real cause of all the harm we receive is our own negativity. If, in such circumstances, we retaliate, we simply create more negative karma and so we shall have to suffer even more harm in the future. If we patiently accept injury, however, we break the chain and that particular karmic debt is paid off.

The patience of voluntarily enduring suffering

If we do not have the patience of voluntarily enduring suffering, we become discouraged whenever we encounter obstacles and whenever our wishes go unfulfilled. We find it hard to complete our tasks because we feel like abandoning them as soon as they become difficult, and our miseries are further aggravated by our impatience. However, it is possible to accept and endure pain if we have a good reason to do so, and whenever we practise such patience we actually reduce our sufferings. For example, if someone were to stick a sharp needle into our flesh, we would find the pain unbearable, but if the needle contained a vaccine that we needed, our tolerance would increase considerably.

Even to succeed in worldly aims, people are prepared to endure adversity. Businessmen sacrifice their leisure and peace of mind just to make money, and soldiers put up with extreme hardship simply to kill other soldiers. How much more willing should we be to bear difficulties for the sake of the most worthwhile aim of all – the attainment of enlightenment for the benefit of all living beings? Because we are in samsara, we often have to endure unpleasant conditions and misfortune. With the patience of voluntarily enduring suffering, however, we can happily and courageously accept these adversities whenever they arise. When our wishes are not fulfilled, or when we are sick, bereaved, or otherwise in difficulty, we should not be discouraged. Instead of feeling self-pity, we should use our suffering to strengthen our spiritual practice. We can recall that all our suffering is the result of our previous negative karma, and resolve to practise pure moral discipline in the future; or we can contemplate that, for as long as we remain in samsara, suffering is inevitable, and thereby increase our renunciation; or we can use our own suffering as an illustration of the much greater suffering experienced by other beings, and in this way strengthen our compassion.

If we are able to endure adversities, we shall reap great rewards. Our present sufferings will diminish, and we shall accomplish both our temporary and our ultimate wishes. Thus, we should not see suffering as an obstacle to our spiritual practice but as an indispensable aid. As Shantideva says:

Moreover, suffering has many good qualities.
Through experiencing it, we can dispel pride,
Develop compassion for those trapped in samsara,
Abandon non-virtue, and delight in virtue.

The patience of definitely thinking about Dharma

If we listen to, contemplate, or meditate on Dharma with a patient and joyful mind so as to gain a special experience of it, we are practising the patience of definitely thinking about Dharma. Such patience is important because if our mind is impatient or unhappy when we engage in Dharma practice, this will obstruct our spiritual progress and prevent us from improving our Dharma wisdom. Even if we find some aspects of our Dharma practice difficult, we still need to engage in them with a happy mind.

THE PERFECTION OF EFFORT

Effort is a mind that delights in virtue. Effort practised with bodhichitta motivation is a perfection of effort. Effort is not something to be practised separately, but a practice that should accompany all our virtuous endeavours. We practise effort when we apply ourself enthusiastically to Dharma study or meditation, strive to accomplish Dharma realizations, or put effort into helping others. Applying ourself energetically to non-virtuous or neutral actions, however, is not a practice of effort.

With effort we can attain mundane and supramundane happiness – it enables us to complete those virtuous

Glorious Array Illuminating All

actions that cause birth in the fortunate realms as well as those that lead to liberation and enlightenment. With effort, we can purify all our negativities and attain whatever good qualities we wish for. However, without effort, even if our wisdom is sharp we shall be unable to complete our spiritual practices.

To generate effort, we need to overcome the three types of laziness: procrastination, attraction to what is meaningless or non-virtuous, and discouragement. Procrastination is a reluctance or unwillingness to put effort into spiritual practice immediately. For example, although we may have an interest in Dharma and intend to practise it, we may feel that we can postpone our practice until some point in the future – when we have had a holiday, when the children have grown up, or when we retire. This is a dangerous attitude because the opportunity to practise Dharma is easily lost. Death can strike at any time. Moreover, when we have finished the particular task that is presently preventing us from practising Dharma, we can be certain that another will arise to take its place. Worldly activities are like an old man's beard – though he may shave it off in the morning, it has grown again by the evening. Therefore, we should abandon procrastination and begin to practise Dharma immediately. The best remedy for the laziness of procrastination is to meditate on our precious human life and on death and impermanence.

Most of us are very familiar with the second type of laziness. We give in to it whenever we watch television for hours on end without caring what comes on, when we indulge in prolonged conversations with no purpose, or when we become engrossed in sports or business ventures for their own sake. Activities such as these dissipate the energy we have for practising Dharma. Though they may seem pleasant, they deceive us – wasting our precious human life and destroying our opportunity to attain real and lasting happiness. To overcome this type of laziness, we need to meditate again and again on the dangers of samsara, remembering that all the entertainments of worldly life are deceptive because in reality they serve only to bind us within samsara and cause us even more suffering.

The laziness of discouragement is very common in these degenerate times. Since we cannot see with our own eyes living examples of enlightened beings, and since our spiritual progress is often much slower than we expect it to be, we may begin to doubt whether Buddhahood is possible, or we may conclude that it must be so rare that there is almost no hope of attaining it. We may also see faults in our Spiritual Guide and in those who are practising Dharma, and conclude that they have no realizations and that effort put into Dharma practice is wasted. If we find we are becoming discouraged in this way, we need to remember that every appearance to the minds of ordinary beings is mistaken because it is contaminated by ignorance. We can be certain that when, through practising Dharma sincerely, we eliminate our ignorance and attain pure minds, pure beings such as Buddhas will definitely appear clearly to us.

If we strive to attain higher realizations before we have mastered the basics, we must expect to become discouraged. We need to understand that even the highest realizations have small beginnings, and learn to value the small experiences of Dharma that we have already attained. Perhaps our attitude towards other people is less biased than it used to be, perhaps we are more patient or less arrogant, or perhaps our faith is stronger. These small improvements are the seeds that will eventually grow into higher realizations and we should cherish them accordingly. We should not expect great changes straightaway. We all have Buddha nature – the potential to attain great enlightenment – and, now that we have met perfect instructions on the Mahayana path, if we practise steadily, without becoming discouraged, eventually we shall definitely attain enlightenment without having to undergo great hardships. So what reason is there to become discouraged?

There are three types of effort: armour-like effort, which is a strong determination to succeed that we generate at the beginning of a virtuous action; the effort of gathering virtuous Dharmas, which is the actual effort we apply when we strive to gain Dharma realizations; and the effort of benefiting others, which is the effort we apply when we strive to benefit other living beings.

We need to apply effort in a skilful way. Some people begin their practice with great enthusiasm and then give up when great results do not appear, like a waterfall caused by a sudden storm cascading furiously for a short time and then trickling away to nothing. Our effort should not be like this. At the very beginning of our practice, we should make a firm decision that we shall persevere until we attain Buddhahood no matter how long it takes, even if it takes many lives. Then we should practise gently and constantly, like a great river that flows day and night, year after year.

When we are tired we should relax, and resume our practice when we are properly rested. If we try to force ourself beyond our natural capacity, we shall only become tense, irritable, or sick. Dharma practice should be a joyful affair. If others see us miserable while we are practising Dharma, they will not believe that Dharma brings peace and happiness. It is said that when we practise Dharma we should be like a child at play. When children are engrossed in their games, they feel completely contented and nothing can distract them.

THE PERFECTION OF MENTAL STABILIZATION

Mental stabilization, or concentration, is a mind whose nature is to be single-pointedly placed on a virtuous object and whose function is to prevent distraction. Any concentration practised with bodhichitta motivation is a perfection of mental stabilization.

Jewel Lotus Great Subduer

For ordinary beings, concentration functions mainly by means of mental awareness. Our sense awarenesses can behold and remain single-pointedly on their objects, but these are not concentrations. For example, when our eye awareness stares single-pointedly at a candle, or our ear awareness becomes absorbed in a piece of music, we are not practising concentration. To improve our concentration so that we attain the nine mental abidings and eventually tranquil abiding, it is necessary for our mind to gather within and dwell upon its object single-pointedly. To accomplish this, we must take as our main object of concentration a generic image, or mental image, that appears to the mental awareness. Eventually, through the power of concentration, the generic image is worn away and the object is perceived directly.

When the sea is rough, sediment is churned up and the water becomes murky, but, when the wind dies down, the mud gradually settles and the water becomes clear. Likewise, in a mind stilled by concentration the delusions subside and the mind becomes extremely lucid. At the moment, our minds are intractable, refusing to cooperate with our virtuous intentions; but concentration melts the tension in our body and mind, and makes them supple, comfortable, and easy to work with. It is difficult for a distracted mind to become sufficiently acquainted with its object to induce spontaneous realizations because it feels as if the mind is 'here' and the object 'there'. A concentrated mind, however, enters into its object and mixes with it, and, as a result, realizations of the stages of the path are quickly attained.

Mental stabilization can be used for either mundane or supramundane purposes. The highest planes within samsara are entered by refining the mind through the practice of concentration. Once a meditator has attained tranquil abiding he can, if he wishes, go on to attain rebirth in the form and formless realms. He or she begins by contemplating the gross and painful nature of the desire realm and the relative peace, purity, and subtlety of the form realm. Gradually he abandons the delusions of the desire realm – principally sensual desire and all forms of anger – so that in his next life he can be reborn as a god of the form realm. If the meditator continues to refine his mind, he will gradually ascend to progressively more and more subtle levels of concentration until eventually he attains the so-called 'concentration of peak of samsara'. With this concentration, he can be reborn in peak of samsara – the highest level of the formless realm and the highest attainment within samsara. Such a rebirth is attained mainly through the force of concentration, without the wisdom realizing emptiness. Some non-Buddhists mistakenly believe this to be a state of liberation but, although at this stage gross delusions have been suppressed, very subtle delusions still have not been eliminated, and so eventually the grosser delusions will arise and once again the meditator will have to descend to lower states.

Only a direct realization of emptiness has the power to cut the continuum of self-grasping, the root of all delusions, and thereby release us from samsara altogether. Therefore, from the beginning, we should train in tranquil abiding with the motivation of renunciation and bodhichitta so that we can overcome self-grasping together with its imprints, and free ourself and all other living beings from the sufferings of samsara.

In earlier times, it was fairly easy to attain tranquil abiding and the form and formless realm absorptions, but nowadays – as our merit decreases, our delusions grow stronger, and distractions abound – these attainments are much more difficult. Therefore, we need to prepare well, especially by overcoming desirous attachment, and then be willing to practise steadily for a long time before we can attain higher levels of concentration.

In the course of mastering the concentrations of the form and formless realms, we attain clairvoyance and other miracle powers. Although these have little meaning in themselves, they can be used by Bodhisattvas to enhance their ability to help others. For example, although we may have very good intentions, sometimes, through not knowing others' minds, we misjudge a situation and our actions prove to be more of a hindrance than a help. Such problems can be overcome by developing a clairvoyance that knows others' minds. However, we should not strive to attain clairvoyance and miracle powers simply for our own sake. If we have taken Bodhisattva vows, we should have a strong interest in improving our concentration only as a means of fulfilling our wish to benefit others. If, having taken Bodhisattva vows, we show no interest in improving our concentration, we incur a secondary downfall.

THE PERFECTION OF WISDOM

Wisdom is a virtuous mind that functions mainly to dispel doubt and confusion by understanding its object thoroughly. Wisdom practised with bodhichitta motivation is a perfection of wisdom.

Wisdom is not the same as worldly intelligence. It is possible to have great intelligence but little wisdom. For example, people who invent weapons of mass destruction are very clever from a worldly point of view, but they have very little wisdom. Similarly, there are people who know a great many facts and understand complex technical subjects, but who have no idea how to maintain a peaceful mind and lead a virtuous life. Such people may have great intelligence, but they have little wisdom.

Wisdom is a special type of understanding that induces peace of mind by clearly distinguishing what is virtuous and to be practised from what is non-virtuous and to be avoided. Wisdom provides our spiritual practice with vision. Without the guidance of wisdom, the other five perfections would be blind, and would not be able to lead us to the final destination of Buddhahood.

A direct realization of ultimate truth, emptiness, can be attained only by a wisdom that is conjoined with tranquil abiding. With a wavering mind, we shall never perceive a subtle object such as emptiness clearly enough to be able to realize it directly, just as we cannot read a book properly by the light of a flickering candle. Training in mental stabilization is like shielding our mind from the winds of distracting thoughts, while wisdom is like the light of the flame itself. When these two are brought together, we attain a clear and powerful perception of the object.

After attaining tranquil abiding, we should strive to attain a union of tranquil abiding and superior seeing observing emptiness. The nature of superior seeing is wisdom. Just as tranquil abiding is a special and superior kind of concentration, so superior seeing is a superior wisdom arising in dependence upon tranquil abiding. When we have attained tranquil abiding, our concentration cannot be disturbed by conceptual thoughts. It is unshakeable, like a huge mountain that cannot be moved by the wind. With such stable concentration, we can investigate our observed object more thoroughly. Through the power of repeated investigation, eventually we shall gain a superior knowledge of the nature of our object of meditation. This wisdom of investigation induces a special mental suppleness. A wisdom that is qualified by such suppleness is superior seeing.

When we first attain superior seeing observing emptiness, our realization of emptiness is still conceptual, but, by continuing to meditate on emptiness with the wisdom of superior seeing, we can gradually eliminate the generic image until finally we perceive emptiness directly, without even a trace of conceptuality.

Since Bodhisattvas wish to become enlightened as quickly as possible, they have a strong wish to accumulate powerful merit quickly. Therefore, they practise each of the six perfections in conjunction with all the others. For example, when Bodhisattvas practise giving, they do so without self-interest, expecting nothing in return. In this way, they practise in accordance with their Bodhisattva vows and combine the perfection of giving with the perfection of moral discipline. By patiently accepting any hardships involved, and not allowing anger to arise if no gratitude is shown, they combine the perfection of giving with the perfection of patience. By giving joyfully, they combine the perfection of giving with the perfection of effort. By concentrating their minds, thinking, 'May the merit of my action of giving enable this person to attain Buddhahood', they combine it with the perfection of mental stabilization. Finally, by realizing that the giver, the gift, and the action of giving all lack inherent existence, they combine the perfection of giving with the perfection of wisdom.

The other perfections can also be practised in this way, with each perfection being practised in conjunction with all the others. This is the armour-like skilful action of a Bodhisattva that hastens the completion of the two collections – the collection of merit and the collection of wisdom – that are the causes of the Form Body and the Truth Body of a Buddha, respectively. Because Bodhisattvas perform all their actions with the motivation of bodhichitta, their whole life is taken up with the practice of the six perfections, and in this way they avoid incurring any of the root and secondary downfalls of the Bodhisattva vows.

King of Mount Meru

The Results

By practising the methods described in this book, we shall eventually attain spontaneous bodhichitta, and from then on the wish to attain Buddhahood for the sake of all living beings will arise naturally day and night. At this point, we shall become a Bodhisattva on the Mahayana path of accumulation.

When, by continuing to train in concentration and wisdom with bodhichitta motivation, we attain the union of tranquil abiding and superior seeing observing emptiness, we become a Bodhisattva on the Mahayana path of preparation; and when, by improving this union, we gain a direct realization of emptiness, we advance to the Mahayana path of seeing. At this stage, we abandon all intellectually-formed delusions. Then, when we attain an uncontaminated wisdom that acts as the direct antidote to the first level of innate delusions, we advance to the Mahayana path of meditation.

By continuing to meditate on emptiness, eventually we attain the vajra-like concentration of the path of meditation, which is the direct antidote to the most subtle obstructions to omniscience and the last mind of a sentient being. In the next moment, we attain the Mahayana Path of No More Learning and become a fully enlightened Buddha. Then our mind will be free from all obstructions, we shall see all past, present, and future phenomena directly and simultaneously, and we shall have the ability to help all living beings by emanating infinite Emanation Bodies.

Dedication

Through the virtues I have created by reading, contemplating, and meditating on these instructions, may all living beings enter into the Bodhisattva's way of life and swiftly accomplish the supreme bliss of full enlightenment.

Appendix I
The Condensed Meaning
of the Commentary

The Condensed Meaning of the Commentary

The commentary, *The Bodhisattva Vow*, has five parts:

1 Introduction
2 The method for receiving and maintaining the Bodhisattva vows
3 The method for completing the vows and trainings of a Bodhisattva
4 The results
5 Dedication

The method for receiving and maintaining the Bodhisattva vows has five parts:

1 Taking the refuge vows
2 Generating bodhichitta
3 Maintaining aspiring bodhichitta by means of ritual
4 Receiving the Bodhisattva vows
5 Maintaining joy and conscientiousness

The method for completing the vows and trainings of a Bodhisattva has three parts:

1 An explanation of the downfalls of the Bodhisattva vows
2 A method for purifying downfalls
3 The actual trainings of a Bodhisattva

An explanation of the downfalls of the Bodhisattva vows has two parts:

1 The forty-six secondary downfalls
2 The eighteen root downfalls

A method for purifying downfalls has two parts:

1 The *Mahayana Sutra of the Three Superior Heaps*
2 An explanation of the practice

An explanation of the practice has three parts:

1 An introduction to the practice
2 The visualization
3 The actual practice

The actual practice has three parts:

1 Purifying non-virtuous actions
2 Dedicating virtue
3 Conclusion

Purifying non-virtuous actions has four parts:

1 The power of reliance
2 The power of the opponent force
3 The power of regret
4 The power of promise

The actual trainings of a Bodhisattva has six parts:

1 The perfection of giving
2 The perfection of moral discipline
3 The perfection of patience
4 The perfection of effort
5 The perfection of mental stabilization
6 The perfection of wisdom

The perfection of giving has three parts:

1 Giving material things
2 Giving Dharma
3 Giving fearlessness

The perfection of moral discipline has three parts:

1 The moral discipline of restraint
2 The moral discipline of gathering virtuous Dharmas
3 The moral discipline of benefiting living beings

The perfection of patience has three parts:

1 The patience of not retaliating
2 The patience of voluntarily enduring suffering
3 The patience of definitely thinking about Dharma

Appendix II
Vows and Commitments

Vows and Commitments

THE REFUGE VOWS

1 Not to go for refuge to teachers who contradict Buddha's view, or to samsaric gods.
2 To regard any image of Buddha as an actual Buddha.
3 Not to harm others.
4 To regard any Dharma scripture as an actual Dharma Jewel.
5 Not to allow ourself to be influenced by people who reject Buddha's teaching.
6 To regard anyone who wears the robes of an ordained person as an actual Sangha Jewel.
7 To go for refuge to the Three Jewels again and again, remembering their good qualities and the differences between them.
8 To offer the first portion of whatever we eat and drink to the Three Jewels, remembering their kindness.
9 With compassion, always to encourage others to go for refuge.
10 Remembering the benefits of going for refuge, to go for refuge at least three times during the day and three times during the night.
11 To perform every action with complete trust in the Three Jewels.
12 Never to forsake the Three Jewels even at the cost of our life, or as a joke.

THE PRECEPTS OF ASPIRING BODHICHITTA

1 To remember the benefits of bodhichitta six times a day.
2 To generate bodhichitta six times a day.
3 Not to abandon any living being.
4 To accumulate merit and wisdom.
5 Not to cheat or deceive our Preceptors or Spiritual Guides.
6 Not to criticize those who have entered the Mahayana.
7 Not to cause others to regret their virtuous actions.
8 Not to pretend to have good qualities or hide our faults without a special, pure intention.

THE ROOT DOWNFALLS OF THE BODHISATTVA VOWS

1 Praising ourself and scorning others.
2 Not giving wealth or Dharma.
3 Not accepting others' apologies.
4 Abandoning the Mahayana.
5 Stealing the property of the Three Jewels.
6 Abandoning Dharma.
7 Taking away saffron robes.
8 Committing the five heinous actions.
9 Holding wrong views.
10 Destroying places such as towns.
11 Explaining emptiness to those who are likely to misunderstand.
12 Causing others to abandon the Mahayana.
13 Causing others to abandon the Pratimoksha.
14 Belittling the Hinayana.
15 Speaking falsely about profound emptiness.
16 Accepting property that has been stolen from the Three Jewels.
17 Making bad rules.
18 Giving up bodhichitta.

THE SECONDARY DOWNFALLS OF THE BODHISATTVA VOWS

1 Not making offerings to the Three Jewels every day.
2 Indulging in worldly pleasures out of attachment.
3 Being disrespectful to those who received the Bodhisattva vows before us.
4 Not replying to others.
5 Not accepting invitations.
6 Not accepting gifts.
7 Not giving Dharma to those who desire it.
8 Forsaking those who have broken their moral discipline.
9 Not acting in ways that cause others to generate faith.
10 Doing little to benefit others.
11 Not believing that Bodhisattvas' compassion ensures that all their actions are pure.
12 Acquiring wealth or fame through wrong livelihood.
13 Indulging in frivolity.
14 Claiming that Bodhisattvas need not abandon samsara.
15 Not avoiding a bad reputation.
16 Not helping others to avoid negativity.
17 Retaliating to harm or abuse.
18 Not apologizing when we have the opportunity.
19 Not accepting others' apologies.
20 Making no effort to control our anger.
21 Gathering a circle of followers out of desire for profit or respect.
22 Not trying to overcome laziness.
23 Indulging in senseless conversation out of attachment.
24 Neglecting to train in mental stabilization.
25 Not overcoming obstacles to mental stabilization.
26 Being preoccupied with the taste of mental stabilization.

27 Abandoning the Hinayana.
28 Studying the Hinayana to the detriment of our Mahayana practice.
29 Studying non-Dharma subjects without a good reason.
30 Becoming engrossed in non-Dharma subjects for their own sake.
31 Criticizing other Mahayana traditions.
32 Praising ourself and scorning others.
33 Making no effort to study Dharma.
34 Preferring to rely upon books rather than upon our Spiritual Guide.
35 Not going to the assistance of those in need.
36 Neglecting to take care of the sick.
37 Not acting to dispel suffering.
38 Not helping others to overcome their bad habits.
39 Not returning help to those who benefit us.
40 Not relieving the distress of others.
41 Not giving to those who seek charity.
42 Not taking special care of disciples.
43 Not acting in accordance with the inclinations of others.
44 Not praising the good qualities of others.
45 Not doing wrathful actions when appropriate.
46 Not using miracle powers, threatening actions, and so forth.

Appendix III
The Letter PAM

Glossary

Attachment A deluded mental factor that observes a contaminated object, regards it as a cause of happiness, and wishes for it. See *Joyful Path of Good Fortune*.

Avalokiteshvara 'Chenrezig' in Tibetan. The embodiment of the compassion of all the Buddhas. At the time of Buddha Shakyamuni, he manifested as a Bodhisattva disciple. See *Tantric Grounds and Paths*.

Awareness All minds are included within the five sense awarenesses and mental awareness. There are five types of sense awareness: eye awareness, ear awareness, nose awareness, tongue awareness, and body awareness. There are two types of mental awareness: conceptual mental awareness and non-conceptual mental awareness. See *Understanding the Mind*.

Beginningless time According to the Buddhist world view, there is no beginning to mind, and so no beginning to time. Therefore, all sentient beings have taken countless previous rebirths.

Blessings The transformation of our mind from a negative state to a positive state, from an unhappy state to a happy state, or from a state of weakness to a state of strength, through the inspiration of holy beings such as our Spiritual Guide, Buddhas, and Bodhisattvas.

Buddhahood Synonymous with full enlightenment. See also *Enlightenment*.

Buddha nature The root mind of a sentient being, and its ultimate nature. Buddha nature, Buddha seed, and Buddha lineage are synonyms. All sentient beings have Buddha nature and therefore the potential to attain Buddhahood.

Buddha's bodies A Buddha has four bodies – the Wisdom Truth Body, the Nature Body, the Enjoyment Body, and the Emanation Body. The first is Buddha's omniscient mind. The second is the emptiness, or ultimate nature, of his or her mind. The third is his subtle Form Body. The fourth, of which each Buddha manifests a countless number, are gross Form Bodies that are visible to ordinary beings. The Wisdom Truth Body and the Nature Body are both included within the Truth Body, and the Enjoyment Body and the Emanation Body are both included within the Form Body. See *Joyful Path of Good Fortune.*

Buddha Shakyamuni The Buddha who is the founder of the Buddhist religion. See *Introduction to Buddhism.*

Buddhist Anyone who from the depths of his or her heart goes for refuge to the Three Jewels – Buddha Jewel, Dharma Jewel, and Sangha Jewel. See *Introduction to Buddhism.*

Chandrakirti (circa 7th century AD) A great Indian Buddhist scholar and meditation master who composed, among many other books, the well-known *Guide to the Middle Way,* in which he clearly elucidates the view of the Madhyamika-Prasangika school according to Buddha's teachings given in the *Perfection of Wisdom Sutras.* See *Ocean of Nectar.*

Clear light A manifest very subtle mind that perceives an appearance like clear, empty space. See *Clear Light of Bliss* and *Tantric Grounds and Paths.*

Compassion A virtuous mind that wishes others to be free from suffering. See also *Great compassion.* See *Joyful Path of Good Fortune.*

Completion stage Highest Yoga Tantra realizations developed in dependence upon the winds entering, abiding, and dissolving within the central channel through the force of meditation. See *Clear Light of Bliss* and *Tantric Grounds and Paths.*

Concentration A mental factor that makes its primary mind remain on its object single-pointedly. Generally, the terms 'mental stabilization' and 'concentration' are interchangeable. More specifically, the term 'concentration' is used to refer to the nature of concentration, which is single-pointedness, and the term 'mental stabilization' is used to refer to the function of concentration, which is stability.

Conceptual mind A thought that apprehends its object through a generic, or mental, image. See *Understanding the Mind*.

Consideration for others A mental factor that functions to avoid inappropriate actions for reasons that concern others. See *Understanding the Mind*.

Degenerate times A period when spiritual activity degenerates.

Delusion A mental factor that arises from inappropriate attention and functions to make the mind unpeaceful and uncontrolled. There are three main delusions: ignorance, desirous attachment, and anger. From these arise all the other delusions, such as jealousy, pride, and deluded doubt. See *Understanding the Mind*.

Demon See *Mara/demon*.

Desire realm The environment of hell beings, hungry ghosts, animals, human beings, demi-gods, and the gods who enjoy the five objects of desire.

Devaputra See *Mara/demon*.

Dharma Buddha's teachings and the inner realizations that are attained in dependence upon practising them. 'Dharma' means 'protection'. By practising Buddha's teachings, we protect ourself from suffering and problems.

Dromtönpa (AD 1004-1064) Atisha's foremost disciple. See *Joyful Path of Good Fortune*.

Emptiness Lack of inherent existence, the ultimate nature of phenomena. See *Heart of Wisdom* and *Ocean of Nectar*.

Enlightenment Any being who has become completely free from the two obstructions, which are the root of all faults, has attained full enlightenment. The two obstructions are the obstructions to liberation (the delusions) and the obstructions to omniscience (the imprints of delusions). See *Joyful Path of Good Fortune*.

Field of Merit The Three Jewels. Just as external seeds grow in a field of soil, so the virtuous internal seeds produced by virtuous actions grow in dependence upon Buddha Jewel, Dharma Jewel, and Sangha Jewel. Also known as 'Field for Accumulating Merit'.

Foe Destroyer 'Arhat' in Sanskrit. A practitioner who has abandoned all delusions and their seeds by training on the spiritual paths, and who will never again be reborn in samsara. In this context, the term 'Foe' refers to the delusions.

Form realm The environment of the gods who possess form.

Formless realm The environment of the gods who do not possess form.

Four ways of gathering disciples The four ways of gathering disciples practised by Bodhisattvas are: (1) pleasing others by giving them material things or whatever they need; (2) teaching Dharma to lead others to liberation; (3) helping others in their Dharma practice by giving them encouragement; and (4) showing others a good example by always practising what we teach.

Generation stage A realization of a creative yoga prior to attaining the actual completion stage, which is attained through the practice of bringing the three bodies into the path, in which one mentally generates oneself as a Tantric Deity and one's surroundings as the Deity's mandala. Meditation on generation stage is called a 'creative yoga' because its object is created, or generated, by correct imagination. See *Tantric Grounds and Paths*.

Generic image The appearing object of a conceptual mind. A generic image, or mental image, of an object is like a reflection of that object. Conceptual minds know their object through the appearance of a generic image of that object, not by seeing the object directly. See *Understanding the Mind*.

Geshe A title given by Kadampa monasteries to accomplished Buddhist scholars. Contracted form of the Tibetan 'ge wai she nyen', literally meaning 'virtuous friend'.

God 'Deva' in Sanskrit. A being of the god realm, the highest of the six realms of samsara. There are many different types of god. Some are desire realm gods, while others are form or formless realm gods. See *Joyful Path of Good Fortune*.

Great compassion A mind wishing to protect all sentient beings from suffering. See *Eight Steps to Happiness*, *Universal Compassion*, and *Ocean of Nectar*.

Happiness There are two types of happiness: mundane and supramundane. Mundane happiness is the limited happiness that can be found within samsara, such as the happiness of humans and gods. Supramundane happiness is the pure happiness of liberation and enlightenment.

Hearer One of two types of Hinayana practitioner. Both Hearers and Solitary Realizers are Hinayanists, but they differ in their motivation, behaviour, merit, and wisdom. In all these respects, Solitary Realizers are superior to Hearers. See *Ocean of Nectar*.

Hell realm The lowest of the six realms of samsara. See *Joyful Path of Good Fortune*.

Hinayana Sanskrit word for 'Lesser Vehicle'. The Hinayana goal is to attain merely one's own liberation from suffering by completely abandoning delusions. See *Joyful Path of Good Fortune*.

Hungry ghost A being of the hungry ghost realm, the second lowest of the six realms of samsara. Also known as 'hungry spirit'. See *Joyful Path of Good Fortune*.

Illusory body The subtle divine body that is principally developed from the indestructible wind. When a practitioner of Highest Yoga Tantra rises from the meditation of the isolated mind of ultimate example clear light, he or she attains a body that is not the same as his or her ordinary physical body. This new body is the illusory body. See *Clear Light of Bliss*.

Imprint There are two types of imprint: imprints of actions and imprints of delusions. Every action we perform leaves an imprint on the mental consciousness, and these imprints are karmic potentialities to experience certain effects in the future. The imprints left by delusions remain even after the delusions themselves have been abandoned, rather as the smell of garlic lingers in a container after the garlic has been removed. Imprints of delusions are obstructions to omniscience, and are completely abandoned only by Buddhas.

Je Tsongkhapa (AD 1357-1419) An emanation of the Wisdom Buddha Manjushri, whose appearance in fourteenth-century Tibet as a monk, and the holder of the lineage of pure view and pure deeds, was prophesied by Buddha. He spread a very pure Buddhadharma throughout Tibet, showing how to combine the practices of Sutra and Tantra, and how to practise pure Dharma during degenerate times. His tradition later became known as the 'Gelug', or 'Ganden Tradition'. See *Heart Jewel* and *Great Treasury of Merit*.

Kadampa A Tibetan word in which 'Ka' means 'word' and refers to all Buddha's teachings, 'dam' refers to Atisha's special Lamrim instructions known as the 'stages of the path to enlightenment', and 'pa' refers to a follower of Kadampa Buddhism who integrates all the teachings of Buddha that they know into their Lamrim practice.

Karma Sanskrit word referring to 'action'. Through the force of intention, we perform actions with our body, speech, and mind, and all of these actions produce effects. The effect of virtuous actions is happiness and the effect of negative actions is suffering. See *Joyful Path of Good Fortune*.

Lamrim A Tibetan term, literally meaning 'stages of the path'. A special arrangement of all Buddha's teachings that is easy to understand and put into practice. It reveals all the stages of the path to enlightenment. For a full commentary, see *Joyful Path of Good Fortune*.

Langri Tangpa, Geshe (AD 1054-1123) A great Kadampa Teacher who was famous for his realization of exchanging self with others. He composed *Eight Verses of Training the Mind*. See *Eight Steps to Happiness*.

Learner Superiors Superior beings who are still training on the learning paths; that is, Superior beings on either the path of seeing or the path of meditation.

Liberation 'Nirvana' in Sanskrit. Complete freedom from samsara and its cause, the delusions. See *Joyful Path of Good Fortune*.

Mahayana Sanskrit word for 'Great Vehicle', the spiritual path to great enlightenment. The Mahayana goal is to attain Buddhahood for the benefit of all sentient beings by completely abandoning delusions and their imprints. See *Joyful Path of Good Fortune*.

Mara/Demon 'Mara' is Sanskrit for 'demon', and refers to anything that obstructs the attainment of liberation or enlightenment. There are four principal types of mara: the mara of the delusions, the mara of contaminated aggregates, the mara of uncontrolled death, and the Devaputra maras. Of these, only the last are actual sentient beings. The principal Devaputra mara is wrathful Ishvara, the highest of the desire realm gods, who inhabits Land of Controlling Emanations. Buddha is called a 'Conqueror' because he or she has conquered all four types of mara. See *Heart of Wisdom*.

Mental stabilization See *Concentration*.

Merit The good fortune created by virtuous actions. It is the potential power to increase our good qualities and produce happiness.

Mind That which is clarity and cognizes. Mind is clarity because it always lacks form and because it possesses the actual power to perceive objects. Mind cognizes because its function is to know or perceive objects. See *Understanding the Mind*.

Nalanda Monastery A great seat of Buddhist learning and practice in ancient India.

Nine mental abidings Nine levels of concentration leading to tranquil abiding: placing the mind, continual placement, replacement, close placement, controlling, pacifying, completely pacifying, single-pointedness, and placement in equipoise. See *Joyful Path of Good Fortune*.

Nirvana See *Liberation.*

Non-conscientiousness A deluded mental factor that wishes to engage in non-virtuous actions without restraint. See *Understanding the Mind.*

Non-virtue A phenomenon that functions as a main cause of suffering. It can refer to non-virtuous minds, non-virtuous actions, non-virtuous imprints, or the ultimate non-virtue of samsara. See *Understanding the Mind.*

Obstructions to liberation Obstructions that prevent the attainment of liberation. All delusions, such as ignorance, attachment, and anger, together with their seeds, are obstructions to liberation. Also called 'delusion-obstructions'.

Obstructions to omniscience The imprints of delusions, which prevent simultaneous and direct realization of all phenomena. Only Buddhas have overcome these obstructions.

Ordinary appearance Any appearance that is due to an impure mind. According to the teachings of Secret Mantra, ordinary appearance is the main cause of samsara. See *Great Treasury of Merit.*

Ordinary conception Any mind that conceives things as ordinary. See *Great Treasury of Merit.*

Preceptor A Spiritual Guide who give us vows or commitments to observe.

Precious human life A life that has eight special freedoms and ten special endowments that make it an ideal opportunity for training the mind in all the stages of the path to enlightenment. See *Joyful Path of Good Fortune.*

Profound path The profound path includes all the wisdom practices that lead to a direct realization of emptiness and ultimately to the Truth Body of a Buddha. See *Joyful Path of Good Fortune.*

Puja A ceremony in which offerings and other acts of devotion are performed in front of holy beings.

Realization A stable and non-mistaken experience of a virtuous object that directly protects us from suffering.

Refuge Actual protection. To go for refuge to Buddha, Dharma, and Sangha means to have faith in these Three Jewels and to rely upon them for protection from all fears and suffering. See *Joyful Path of Good Fortune*.

Renunciation The wish to be released from samsara. See *Joyful Path of Good Fortune*.

Samsara This can be understood in two ways – as uninterrupted rebirth without freedom or control, or as the aggregates of a being who has taken such a rebirth. Samsara is characterized by suffering and dissatisfaction. There are six realms of samsara. Listed in ascending order according to the type of karma that causes rebirth in them, they are the realms of the hell beings, hungry ghosts, animals, human beings, demi-gods, and gods. The first three are lower realms or unhappy migrations, and the second three are higher realms or happy migrations. Although from the point of view of the karma that causes rebirth there, the god realm is the highest realm in samsara, the human realm is said to be the most fortunate realm because it provides the best conditions for attaining liberation and enlightenment. See *Joyful Path of Good Fortune*.

Sangha According to the Vinaya tradition, any community of four or more fully ordained monks or nuns. In general, ordained or lay people who take Bodhisattva vows or Tantric vows can also be said to be Sangha.

Self-cherishing A mental attitude that considers oneself to be supremely important and precious. It is regarded as a principal object to be abandoned by Bodhisattvas. See *Eight Steps to Happiness*.

Self-grasping A conceptual mind that holds any phenomenon to be inherently existent. The mind of self-grasping gives rise to all other delusions, such as anger and attachment. It is the root cause of all suffering and dissatisfaction. See *Heart of Wisdom*.

Sense of shame A mental factor that functions to avoid inappropriate actions for reasons that concern oneself. See *Understanding the Mind*.

Shantideva (AD 687-763) A great Indian Buddhist scholar and meditation master. He composed *Guide to the Bodhisattva's Way of Life*. See *Meaningful to Behold*.

Solitary peace A Hinayana nirvana.

Solitary Realizer A type of Hinayana practitioner. Also known as 'Solitary Conqueror'. See also *Hearer*. See *Ocean of Nectar*.

Spiritual Guide 'Guru' in Sanskrit, 'Lama' in Tibetan. A Teacher who guides us along the spiritual path. See *Joyful Path of Good Fortune* and *Great Treasury of Merit*.

Stages of the path See *Lamrim*.

Sugata Another term for a Buddha. It indicates that Buddhas have attained a state of immaculate and indestructible bliss.

Superior being 'Arya' in Sanskrit. A being who has a direct realization of emptiness. There are Hinayana Superiors and Mahayana Superiors.

Superior seeing A special wisdom that sees its object clearly, and that is maintained by tranquil abiding and the special suppleness that is induced by investigation. See *Joyful Path of Good Fortune*.

Sutra The teachings of Buddha that are open to everyone to practise without the need for empowerment. These include Buddha's teachings of the three turnings of the Wheel of Dharma.

Tantra Tantric teachings are distinguished from Sutra teachings in that they reveal methods for training the mind by bringing the future result, or Buddhahood, into the present path. Tantric practitioners overcome ordinary appearances and conceptions by visualizing their body, environment, enjoyments, and deeds as those of a Buddha. Tantra is the supreme path to full enlightenment. Tantric practices are to be done in private and only by those who have received a

Tantric empowerment. Synonymous with 'Secret Mantra'. See *Tantric Grounds and Paths*.

Tantric bodhichitta A wish to attain enlightenment as a Tantric Deity in order to rescue sentient beings from samsara as quickly as possible.

Ten directions The four cardinal directions, the four intermediate directions, and the directions above and below.

Three Jewels The three objects of refuge: Buddha Jewel, Dharma Jewel, and Sangha Jewel. They are called 'Jewels' because they are both rare and precious. See *Joyful Path of Good Fortune*.

Three times, the Past, present, and future.

Tranquil abiding A concentration that possesses the special bliss of physical and mental suppleness that is attained in dependence upon completing the nine mental abidings. See *Joyful Path of Good Fortune*.

Vast path The vast path includes all the method practices from the initial cultivation of compassion through to the final attainment of the Form Body of a Buddha. See *Joyful Path of Good Fortune*.

Vasubhandu A great Indian Buddhist scholar of the fifth century who was converted to the Mahayana by his older brother, Asanga. He wrote *Treasury of Abhidharma* (Skt. *Abhidharmakosha*).

Vinaya Sutras Sutras in which Buddha principally explains the practice of moral discipline, and in particular the Pratimoksha moral discipline.

Virtue A phenomenon that functions as a main cause of happiness. It can refer to virtuous minds, virtuous actions, virtuous imprints, or the ultimate virtue of nirvana. See *Understanding the Mind*.

Bibliography

Geshe Kelsang Gyatso is a highly respected meditation master and scholar of the Mahayana Buddhist tradition founded by Je Tsong-khapa. Since arriving in the West in 1977, Geshe Kelsang has worked tirelessly to establish pure Buddhadharma throughout the world. Over this period, he has given extensive teachings on the major scriptures of the Mahayana. These teachings are currently being published and provide a comprehensive presentation of the essential Sutra and Tantra practices of Mahayana Buddhism.

Books

The following books by Geshe Kelsang are all published by Tharpa Publications.

The Bodhisattva Vow. The essential practices of Mahayana Buddhism. (2nd. edn., 1995)

Clear Light of Bliss. The practice of Mahamudra in Vajrayana Buddhism. (2nd. edn., 1992)

Eight Steps to Happiness. The Buddhist way of loving kindness. (2000)

Essence of Vajrayana. The Highest Yoga Tantra practice of Heruka body mandala. (1997)

Great Treasury of Merit. The practice of relying upon a Spiritual Guide. (1992)

Guide to Dakini Land. The Highest Yoga Tantra practice of Buddha Vajrayogini. (2nd. edn., 1996)

Guide to the Bodhisattva's Way of Life. How to enjoy a life of great meaning and altruism. (A translation of Shantideva's famous verse masterpiece.) (2002)

Heart Jewel. The essential practices of Kadampa Buddhism. (2nd. edn., 1997)

Heart of Wisdom. An explanation of the *Heart Sutra.* (4th. edn., 2001)

Introduction to Buddhism. An explanation of the Buddhist way of
  life. (2nd. edn., 2001)
Joyful Path of Good Fortune. The complete Buddhist path to
  enlightenment. (2nd. edn., 1995)
Living Meaningfully, Dying Joyfully. The profound practice of
  transference of consciousness. (1999)
Meaningful to Behold. The Bodhisattva's way of life.
  (4th. edn., 1994)
The Meditation Handbook. A practical guide to Buddhist meditation.
  (3rd. edn., 1995)
Ocean of Nectar. Wisdom and compassion in Mahayana
  Buddhism. (1995)
Tantric Grounds and Paths. How to enter, progress on, and
  complete the Vajrayana path. (1994)
Transform Your Life. A blissful journey. (2001)
Understanding the Mind. An explanation of the nature and
  functions of the mind. (2nd. edn., 1997)
Universal Compassion. Transforming your life through love and
  compassion. (4th. edn., 2002)

Sadhanas

Geshe Kelsang has also supervised the translation of a collection of
essential sadhanas, or prayer booklets.

Assembly of Good Fortune. The tsog offering for Heruka body
  mandala.
Avalokiteshvara Sadhana. Prayers and requests to the Buddha of
  Compassion.
The Bodhisattva's Confession of Moral Downfalls. The purification
  practice of the *Mahayana Sutra of the Three Superior Heaps*.
Condensed Essence of Vajrayana. Condensed Heruka body mandala
  self-generation sadhana.
Dakini Yoga. Six-session Guru yoga combined with
  self-generation as Vajrayogini.
Drop of Essential Nectar. A special fasting and purification
  practice in conjunction with Eleven-faced Avalokiteshvara.
Essence of Good Fortune. Prayers for the six preparatory practices
  for meditation on the stages of the path to enlightenment.
Essence of Vajrayana. Heruka body mandala self-generation
  sadhana according to the system of Mahasiddha Ghantapa.
Feast of Great Bliss. Vajrayogini self-initiation sadhana.

Great Compassionate Mother. The sadhana of Arya Tara.

Great Liberation of the Mother. Preliminary prayers for Mahamudra meditation in conjunction with Vajrayogini practice.

The Great Mother. A method to overcome hindrances and obstacles by reciting the *Essence of Wisdom Sutra* (the *Heart Sutra*).

Heartfelt Prayers. Funeral service for cremations and burials.

Heart Jewel. The Guru yoga of Je Tsongkhapa combined with the condensed sadhana of his Dharma Protector.

The Hundreds of Deities of the Joyful Land. The Guru yoga of Je Tsongkhapa.

The Kadampa Way of Life. The essential practice of Kadam Lamrim.

Liberation from Sorrow. Praises and requests to the Twenty-one Taras.

Mahayana Refuge Ceremony and Bodhisattva Vow Ceremony.

Medicine Buddha Sadhana. The method for making requests to the Assembly of Seven Medicine Buddhas.

Meditation and Recitation of Solitary Vajrasattva.

Melodious Drum Victorious in all Directions. The extensive fulfilling and restoring ritual of the Dharma Protector, the great king Dorje Shugdän, in conjunction with Mahakala, Kalarupa, Kalindewi, and other Dharma Protectors.

Offering to the Spiritual Guide (*Lama Chöpa*). A special Guru yoga practice of Je Tsongkhapa's tradition.

Pathway to the Pure Land. Training in powa – the transference of consciousness.

Prayers for Meditation. Brief preparatory prayers for meditation.

A Pure Life. The practice of taking and keeping the eight Mahayana precepts.

The Quick Path. A condensed practice of Heruka Five Deities according to Master Ghantapa's tradition.

Quick Path to Great Bliss. Vajrayogini self-generation sadhana.

Treasury of Blessings. The condensed meaning of Vajrayana Mahamudra and prayers of request to the lineage Gurus.

Treasury of Wisdom. The sadhana of Venerable Manjushri.

Vajra Hero Yoga. A brief essential practice of Heruka body mandala self-generation, and condensed six-session yoga.

The Vows and Commitments of Kadampa Buddhism.

Wishfulfilling Jewel. The Guru yoga of Je Tsongkhapa combined with the sadhana of his Dharma Protector.

The Yoga of Buddha Amitayus. A special method for increasing lifespan, wisdom, and merit.

The Yoga of White Tara, Buddha of Long Life.

To order any of our publications, or to
receive a catalogue, please contact:

Tharpa Publications
Conishead Priory
Ulverston
Cumbria LA12 9QQ
England

Tel: 01229-588599
Fax: 01229-483919

E-mail: tharpa@tharpa.com
Website: www.tharpa.com

or

Tharpa Publications
47 Sweeney Road
P.O. Box 430
Glen Spey, NY 12737
USA

Tel: 845-856-5102 or
888-741-3475 (toll free)
Fax: 845-856-2110

Email: tharpa-us@tharpa.com
Website: www.tharpa.com

Study Programmes of Kadampa Buddhism

Kadampa Buddhism is a Mahayana Buddhist school founded by the great Indian Buddhist Master Atisha (AD 982-1054). His followers are known as 'Kadampas'. 'Ka' means 'word' and refers to Buddha's teachings, and 'dam' refers to Atisha's special Lamrim instructions known as 'the stages of the path to enlightenment'. By integrating their knowledge of all Buddha's teachings into their practice of Lamrim, and by integrating this into their everyday lives, Kadampa Buddhists are encouraged to use Buddha's teachings as practical methods for transforming daily activities into the path to enlightenment. The great Kadampa Teachers are famous not only for being great scholars, but also for being spiritual practitioners of immense purity and sincerity.

The lineage of these teachings, both their oral transmission and blessings, was then passed from Teacher to disciple, spreading throughout much of Asia, and now to many countries throughout the Western world. Buddha's teachings, which are known as 'Dharma', are likened to a wheel that moves from country to country in accordance with changing conditions and people's karmic inclinations. The external forms of presenting Buddhism may change as it meets with different cultures and societies, but its essential authenticity is ensured through the continuation of an unbroken lineage of realized practitioners.

Kadampa Buddhism was first introduced into the West in 1977 by the renowned Buddhist Master, Venerable Geshe Kelsang Gyatso. Since that time, he has worked tirelessly to spread Kadampa Buddhism throughout the world by giving extensive teachings, writing many profound texts on Kadampa Buddhism, and founding the New Kadampa Tradition (NKT), which now has over four hundred Kadampa Buddhist Centres worldwide. Each Centre offers study programmes on Buddhist psychology, philosophy, and meditation instruction, as well as retreats for all levels of practitioner. The emphasis is on integrating Buddha's teachings into daily life to solve our human problems and to spread lasting peace and happiness throughout the world.

The Kadampa Buddhism of the NKT is an entirely independent Buddhist tradition and has no political affiliations. It is an association of Buddhist Centres and practitioners that derive their inspiration and guidance from the example of the ancient Kadampa Buddhist Masters and their teachings, as presented by Geshe Kelsang.

There are three reasons why we need to study and practise the teachings of Buddha: to develop our wisdom, to cultivate a good heart, and to maintain a peaceful state of mind. If we do not strive to develop our wisdom, we will always remain ignorant of ultimate truth – the true nature of reality. Although we wish for happiness, our ignorance leads us to engage in non-virtuous actions, which are the main cause of all our suffering. If we do not cultivate a good heart, our selfish motivation destroys harmony and good relationships with others. We have no peace, and no chance to gain pure happiness. Without inner peace, outer peace is impossible. If we do not maintain a peaceful state of mind, we are not happy even if we have ideal conditions. On the other hand, when our mind is peaceful, we are happy, even if our external conditions are unpleasant. Therefore, the development of these qualities is of utmost importance for our daily happiness.

Geshe Kelsang Gyatso, or 'Geshe-la' as he is affectionately called by his students, has designed three special spiritual programmes for the systematic study and practice of Kadampa Buddhism that are especially suited to the modern world – the General Programme (GP), the Foundation Programme (FP), and the Teacher Training Programme (TTP).

GENERAL PROGRAMME

The General Programme provides a basic introduction to Buddhist view, meditation, and practice that is suitable for beginners. It also includes advanced teachings and practice from both Sutra and Tantra.

FOUNDATION PROGRAMME

The Foundation Programme provides an opportunity to deepen our understanding and experience of Buddhism through a systematic study of five texts:

1 *Joyful Path of Good Fortune* – a commentary to Atisha's Lamrim instructions, the stages of the path to enlightenment.
2 *Universal Compassion* – a commentary to Bodhisattva Chekhawa's *Training the Mind in Seven Points*.

3 *Heart of Wisdom* – a commentary to the *Heart Sutra*.
4 *Meaningful to Behold* – a commentary to Venerable Shantideva's *Guide to the Bodhisattva's Way of Life*.
5 *Understanding the Mind* – a detailed explanation of the mind, based on the works of the Buddhist scholars Dharmakirti and Dignaga.

The benefits of studying and practising these texts are as follows:

(1) *Joyful Path of Good Fortune* – we gain the ability to put all Buddha's teachings of both Sutra and Tantra into practice. We can easily make progress on, and complete, the stages of the path to the supreme happiness of enlightenment. From a practical point of view, Lamrim is the main body of Buddha's teachings, and the other teachings are like its limbs.

(2) *Universal Compassion* – we gain the ability to integrate Buddha's teachings into our daily life and solve all our human problems.

(3) *Heart of Wisdom* – we gain a realization of the ultimate nature of reality. By gaining this realization, we can eliminate the ignorance of self-grasping, which is the root of all our suffering.

(4) *Meaningful to Behold* – we transform our daily activities into the Bodhisattva's way of life, thereby making every moment of our human life meaningful.

(5) *Understanding the Mind* – we understand the relationship between our mind and its external objects. If we understand that objects depend upon the subjective mind, we can change the way objects appear to us by changing our own mind. Gradually, we will gain the ability to control our mind and in this way solve all our problems.

TEACHER TRAINING PROGRAMME

The Teacher Training Programme is designed for people who wish to train as authentic Dharma Teachers. In addition to completing the study of twelve texts of Sutra and Tantra, which include the five texts mentioned above, the student is required to observe certain commitments with regard to behaviour and way of life, and to complete a number of meditation retreats.

All Kadampa Buddhist Centres are open to the public. Every year we celebrate Festivals in the USA and Europe, including two in England, where people gather from around the world to receive special teachings and empowerments and to enjoy a spiritual vacation. Please feel free to visit us at any time!

For further information, please contact:

UK NKT Office
Conishead Priory
Ulverston
Cumbria LA12 9QQ
England

Tel/Fax: 01229-588533

Email: kadampa@dircon.co.uk
Website: www.kadampa.org

or

US NKT Office
Kadampa Meditation Center
47 Sweeney Road
P.O. Box 447
Glen Spey, NY 12737
USA

Tel: 845-856-9000
Fax: 845-856-2110

Email: kadampacenter@aol.com
Website: www.kadampacenter.org

Index

*Collection of Precious Jewels
Sutra* 45
collection of wisdom 105
compassion (see also great
compassion) 17, 23, 94, g
Compendium of Trainings 4, 29
completion stage 5, 6, g
concentration 21, 33, 99-103, g
conceptual mind 104, g
*Condensed Perfection of Wisdom
Sutra* 86
confession 61-5, 74
conscientiousness 11, 69, 85
consideration for others 32, g

D

death 1, 97
dedication 69-74, 108
degenerate times 98, g
delusions 5, 35, 49, 93, 102,
107, g
demon g
desire realm 102, g
Devaputra 51, g
Dharma 15, 21, 22-3, 29, 97,
98, 99, 134-5, g
giving 82
Dharma Jewel 53, 57
disciples 19, 25, 49, 71
downfalls 3, 4, 5, 10-11, 103, 105
Pratimoksha 5, 55
Bodhisattva 5, 13-34, 55, 86,
87
Tantric 5, 55
method for purifying 35-75
Dromtönpa 27, g

E

eight unfree states 63, 65
emptiness 6, 31, 32, 51, 102,
104, 107, g

enlightenment (see also
Buddhahood) 18, 33, g
exalted wisdom 41, 43, 67, 71,
74

F

faith 17, 35, 53
Field for Accumulating Merit
7, g
five heinous actions 31, 65
Foe Destroyer 61, 65, 73, g
form realm 102, g
formless realm 102, g
four binding factors 32
four doors of receiving
downfalls 5
four opponent powers 55, 57
reliance 55, 57-9
opponent force 55, 59-61
regret 55, 61-7
promise 57, 67-9
four ways of gathering
disciples 71, g

G

generation stage 5, 6, g
generic image 101, 104, g
Geshe 27, g
giving (see perfection of giving)
god 47, 65, 102, g
great compassion 1, 87, g
*Guide to the Bodhisattva's Way of
Life* 4, 35

H

happiness 3, 95, g
Hearer 9, g
hell 63, 65, g
Hinayana 17, 21, 29, 32, 71, g
hungry ghost 65, g

Further Reading

JOYFUL PATH OF GOOD FORTUNE
The complete Buddhist path to enlightenment

Step-by-step guidance on all the meditations that lead to limitless peace and happiness. Enriched with stories and analogies, the author presents with great clarity all Buddha's teachings in the order in which they are practised. Following these instructions, we will come to experience for ourselves the joy that arises from making progress on a clear and structured path to enlightenment.

"This book is invaluable." *World Religions in Education.*

MEANINGFUL TO BEHOLD
The Bodhisattva's way of life

Many people have the compassionate wish to benefit others, but few understand how to make this wish effective in their daily life. In this highly acclaimed commentary to the great Buddhist classic *Guide to the Bodhisattva's Way of Life*, the author shows how we can engage in the actual methods that lead to lasting benefit for ourself and others.

"An indispensable Buddhist work – no serious student of Buddhism can afford to be without it." *John Blofeld.*

INTRODUCTION TO BUDDHISM
An explanation of the Buddhist way of life

This book presents the central principles behind the Buddhist way of life, such as meditation and karma, as tools for developing qualities such as inner peace, love, and patience. Those developing an interest in Buddhism and meditation will find this book an ideal guide.

"A brilliantly clear and concise introduction to this vast subject. Very highly recommended." *Yoga & Health Magazine.*